**LEARNER ACTIVITIES WORKBOOK**

# VISIONARY LEADERSHIP
## in Healthcare

### Excellence in Practice, Policy, and Ethics

Holly Wei, PhD, RN, NEA-BC, FAAN
Sara Horton-Deutsch, PhD, RN, PMHCNS, FAAN, ANEF

**Sigma**
GLOBAL NURSING
EXCELLENCE

*Sigma Theta Tau International Honor Society of Nursing (Sigma) is a nonprofit organization whose mission is developing nurse leaders anywhere to improve healthcare everywhere. Founded in 1922, Sigma has more than 135,000 active members in over 100 countries and territories. Members include practicing nurses, instructors, researchers, policymakers, entrepreneurs, and others. Sigma's more than 540 chapters are located at more than 700 institutions of higher education throughout Armenia, Australia, Botswana, Brazil, Canada, Colombia, Croatia, England, Eswatini, Ghana, Hong Kong, Ireland, Israel, Italy, Jamaica, Japan, Jordan, Kenya, Lebanon, Malawi, Mexico, the Netherlands, Nigeria, Pakistan, Philippines, Portugal, Puerto Rico, Scotland, Singapore, South Africa, South Korea, Sweden, Taiwan, Tanzania, Thailand, the United States, and Wales. Learn more at www.sigmanursing.org.*

Sigma Theta Tau International
550 West North Street
Indianapolis, IN, USA 46202

To request a review copy for course adoption, order additional books, buy in bulk, or purchase for corporate use, contact Sigma Marketplace at 888.654.4968 (US/Canada toll-free), +1.317.687.2256 (International), or solutions@sigmamarketplace.org.

To request author information, or for speaker or other media requests, contact Sigma Marketing at 888.634.7575 (US/Canada toll-free) or +1.317.634.8171 (International).

ISBN:        9781646480647
PDF ISBN:    9781646480661

First Printing, 2022

**Publisher:** Dustin Sullivan                     **Managing Editor:** Carla Hall
**Acquisitions Editor:** Emily Hatch                **Publications Specialist:** Todd Lothery
**Development Editor:** Jill Stanley                 **Project Editor:** Jill Stanley
**Cover Designer:** Michael Tanamachi               **Copy Editor:** Erin Geile
**Interior Design/Page Layout:** Rebecca Batchelor   **Proofreader:** Todd Lothery

# ABOUT THE LEAD AUTHORS

**Holly Wei, PhD, RN, NEA-BC, FAAN,** is a Professor and Assistant Dean for the PhD program at the University of Louisville School of Nursing. Her overarching research focuses on healthcare organizational culture, leadership development, clinician well-being, stress genomic biomarkers, and patient care quality. She is known nationally and internationally for her nursing practice models and a Convergent Care Theory. Multiple healthcare systems have used Wei's nursing models to guide practice and promote organizational culture and patient care with significant improvements in nursing practice and patient care quality.

Wei's scholarly work has reached and influenced the nursing profession in academia and clinical nursing practice globally. In the past five years, Wei had 50 peer-reviewed publications and delivered over 70 presentations, including radio and TV interviews, influencing tens of thousands of nurses globally. Some of her articles are within the top-read, top-downloaded, and top-cited articles of journals. Wei is an Associate Editor of the *International Journal for Human Caring*. She sits on two boards of directors and two journals' editorial board positions, including *Advances in Nursing Science*.

Wei has received numerous prestigious awards throughout her career. Recently, she received the International Leininger Caring-Culture Award, Board of Governors Distinguished Professor for Teaching, DAISY Extraordinary Faculty, Nurse Educator of the Year, Scholar-Teacher Award, Outstanding Research Scholar Award, and Nursing Research Award. These awards affirm her significant contributions and influences in nursing leadership and practice regionally and globally.

**Sara Horton-Deutsch, PhD, RN, PMHCNS, FAAN, ANEF,** is a Caritas Coach and a Professor and the Director of the Kaiser Permanente/USF Partnership at the University of San Francisco, where she mentors the next generation of nursing leaders through the lens of Caring Science and values-based leadership. She also serves as a Faculty Associate with the Watson Caring Science Institute. In 2021, she co-created and initiated the Caritas Leadership Program, a uniquely customized six-month program guiding participants through executive Caring Science leader dialogues, interactive circles, and participant transformation projects. She is also a founding partner of Better Together Healing, LLC, a holistic practice partnership specializing in an integrative approach to heal the self, build collaborations, and create healthy and bounded communities. As a therapeutic practitioner and Caritas leadership coach, she collaborates with healthcare professionals and organizations seeking balance and growth who are open to engaging in innovative approaches to healing. Her comprehensive approach includes certifications in professional coaching and training through the Leadership Circle and Working with Resilience, providing comprehensive profiles and assessments to raise the conscious practice of leadership and build regenerative success at work.

Horton-Deutsch holds a research fellowship at the University of South Africa School of Human Sciences, where she encourages critical discourse and collaborates with faculty to enhance research and scholarship. Her research foci are on leadership development, reflective practice, and creating healing and healthy work environments. She has co-edited four textbooks. Her work has been published in three books with Sigma: *Reflective Practice: Transforming Education and Improving Outcomes* (2012 & 2017), *Reflective Organizations: On the Front Lines of QSEN & Reflective Practice Implementation* (2015), and *Caritas Coaching: A Journey Toward Transpersonal Caring for Informed Moral Action in Healthcare* (2018).

Her most recent awards, honors, and fellowships include 2020–2021 Experienced Academic Nurse Leadership Academy Faculty Mentor, Sigma; 2018–2019 Faculty Fellowship in Ignatian Tradition, University of San Francisco; 2016–2024 Invited Research Fellow, University of South Africa, Johannesburg, South Africa; 2016–2017 Nurse Faculty Leadership Academy, Faculty Mentor, Sigma; 2014 Fellow, American Academy of Nursing; 2013 Fellow, Academy of Nursing Education; Fellow, National League for Nursing.

# CONTRIBUTING AUTHORS

(For expanded bios, see this book's page on the Sigma Repository: http://hdl.handle.net/10755/22206)

**Stephanie Wilkie Ahmed, DNP, NP-BC,** is Associate Chief Nursing Officer and Watson Caring Science Scholar in Residence in the University of Miami Health System.

**Mary Jo Assi, DNP, RN, NEA-BC, FAAN,** is Associate Chief Nursing Officer and Partner, Strategic Consulting, at Press Ganey.

**Nancy M. Ballard, PhD, RN, NEA-BC,** is Assistant Professor at Kennesaw State University.

**Mark D. Beck, DNP, MSN, BS, RN,** is Assistant Professor and Interim Program Director at Samuel Merritt University.

**Wanda J. Borges, PhD, RN, ANP-BC,** is Dean and Professor, and Associate Director of Graduate Programs in the School of Nursing at New Mexico State University.

**Sylvia T. Brown, EdD, RN, CNE, ANEF,** is Dean and Professor at the East Carolina University College of Nursing.

**Chantal Cara, PhD, RN, FAAN, FCAN,** is Professor at Université de Montréal and a Distinguished Caring Science Scholar at the Watson Caring Science Institute.

**Laura Caramanica, PhD, RN, CNE, CNEP, FACHE, FAAN,** is Graduate Program Director and Professor at the University of West Georgia.

**Gabrielle Dawn Childs, MA, MPH, RN,** is a PhD Candidate at the American Graduate School in Paris and a Program Manager for the Peace Corps' Advancing Health Professionals program.

**Peggy L. Chinn, PhD, DSc(Hon), RN, FAAN,** is the Editor of the journal *Advances in Nursing Science* and Professor Emerita at the University of Connecticut.

**Carey S. Clark, PhD, RN, AHN-BSC RYT, FAAN,** is Professor and Director of Nursing at Pacific College of Health and Science.

**Jim D'Alfonso, DNP, PhD(h), RN, NEA-BC, FNAP, FAAN,** is Executive Director, Professional Excellence and the KP Scholars Academy, & Adjunct Faculty at the University of San Francisco.

**Erica DeKruyter, MSN, RN,** is Manager of Educational Resources at Sigma Theta Tau International Honor Society of Nursing (Sigma).

**Jennifer J. Doering, PhD, RN,** is Associate Dean for Academic Affairs and Associate Professor at the University of Wisconsin-Milwaukee College of Nursing.

**Diana Drake, DNP, APRN, WHNP, FAAN, FNAP,** is Clinical Professor and Director of the Women's Health Gender-Related Nurse Practitioner specialty at the University of Minnesota School of Nursing.

**Karen J. Foli, PhD, RN, FAAN,** is Associate Professor in the Purdue University School of Nursing.

**Lynn Gallagher-Ford, PhD, RN, NE-BC, DPFNAP, FAAN/Evidence-based Practice (CH),** is Chief Operating Officer and Director of the Helene Fuld National Trust Institute for Evidence-based Practice in Nursing and Healthcare at the Ohio State University College of Nursing.

**Stephanie D. Gingerich, DNP, RN, CPN,** is Clinical Assistant Professor at the University of Minnesota School of Nursing.

**Kaboni Whitney Gondwe, PhD, RN,** is Assistant Professor at the University of Wisconsin-Milwaukee College of Nursing.

**Ernest J. Grant, PhD, RN, FAAN,** is President of the American Nurses Association.

**Sarah E. Gray, DNP, RN, CEN, FAEN,** is Director of Educational Resources, Global Initiatives, and Marketplace at Sigma Theta Tau International Honor Society of Nursing (Sigma).

**Christine Griffin, PhD, RN, NPD-BC, CPN,** is a Caritas Coach and Professional Development Specialist at Children's Hospital Colorado.

**Senem Guney, PhD,** is Vice President of Language Analytics for Press Ganey.

**Sonya R. Hardin, PhD, CCRN, NP-C, FAAN,** is Dean and Professor at the University of Louisville.

**Grissel Hernandez, PhD, RN, MPH, HNB-BC, NPD-BC, SGAHN,** is Executive Director at Stanford Health Care's Center for Education and Professional Development.

**Marcia Hills, PhD, RN, FAAN, CFAN,** is Professor and Associate Director of Research and Scholarship at the University of Victoria's School of Nursing.

**Phyllis N. Horns, PhD, RN, FAAN,** is Professor of Nursing and Director of the East Carolina Consortium for Nursing Leadership at the East Carolina University College of Nursing.

**Matthew S. Howard, DNP, RN, CEN, TCRN, CPEN, CPN,** is Director of Scholarship and Leadership Resources at Sigma Theta Tau International Honor Society of Nursing (Sigma).

**Rachel Johnson-Koenke, PhD, LCSW,** is Assistant Professor at the University of Colorado College of Nursing.

**Christie Kerwan, MSN, RN,** is Director of Strategic Partnerships—Healthcare for PowerDMS.

**Judy Ngele Khanyola, MSc, BSN, RN,** is Chair for the Center for Nursing and Midwifery at the University of Global Health Equity in Rwanda.

**Carol Ann King, DNP, MSN, BSN, RN, FNP-BC, NHDP-BC,** is Clinical Professor in the Doctor of Nursing Practice–Family and Adult-Gerontology Nurse Practitioner programs at East Carolina University.

**Dame Donna Kinnair, MA, RGN, HV, LLB, PGCE,** is Chief Executive and General Secretary of the Royal College of Nursing in the UK.

**Wipada Kunaviktikul, PhD, RN, RM, FAAN,** is Professor Emerita and Assistant to the President of Health Science Academic Affairs at Panyapiwat Institute of Management in Thailand.

**Donna Lake, PhD, RN, NEA-BC, FAAN,** is Clinical Professor at the East Carolina University College of Nursing.

**Jeneile Luebke PhD, RN,** is a post-doctoral Nurse Research Fellow at the University of Wisconsin-Madison.

**Elizabeth A. Madigan, PhD, RN, FAAN,** is Chief Executive Officer of Sigma Theta Tau International Honor Society of Nursing (Sigma).

**Kathy Malloch, PhD, MBA, RN, FAAN,** is Clinical Professor at the Ohio State University College of Nursing.

**Lucy Mkandawire-Valhmu, PhD, RN,** is Associate Professor at the University of Wisconsin-Milwaukee College of Nursing.

**Chelsie Monroe, MSN, APRN, PMHNP-BC,** is a Psychiatric Mental Health Nurse Practitioner and Owner of Balanced Mental Wellness in Colorado.

**Melissa T. Ojemeni, PhD, RN,** is Director of Nursing Education, Research and Professional Development for Partners In Health in Boston.

**Crystal Oldman, EdD, MSc, MA, RN, RHV, QN, FRCN, CBE,** is Chief Executive at the Queen's Nursing Institute in the UK.

**Danielle EK Perkins, PhD, RN,** is the former Manager of the Center for Excellence in Nursing Education at Sigma Theta Tau International Honor Society of Nursing (Sigma).

**Daniel J. Pesut, PhD, RN, FAAN,** is Emeritus Professor at the University of Minnesota School of Nursing and Emeritus Katherine R. and C. Walton Lillehei Chair of Nursing Leadership at the University of Minnesota.

**Tim Porter-O'Grady, DM, EdD, ScD(h), APRN, FAAN, FACCWS,** is Senior Partner for Tim Porter-O'Grady Associates LLC & Clinical Professor at the Emory University School of Nursing.

**Teddie M. Potter, PhD, RN, FAAN, FNAP,** is Clinical Professor, Director of Planetary Health, and Coordinator of the Doctor of Nursing Practice in Health Innovation and Leadership program at the University of Minnesota School of Nursing.

**Katherine Reed, LPC,** is Program Manager of the Ponzio Creative Arts Therapy program at Children's Hospital Colorado.

**Jennifer Reese, MD,** is Associate Professor of Clinical Pediatrics at the University of Colorado School of Medicine and Section Head of the Pediatric Hospital Medicine.

**William E. Rosa, PhD, MBE, NP-BC, FAANP, FAAN,** is Chief Research Fellow at Memorial Sloan Kettering Cancer Center's Department of Psychiatry and Behavioral Sciences.

**Barbara Sattler, DrPH, RN, FAAN,** is Professor Emerita at the University of San Francisco School of Nursing and Health Professions.

**Gwen Sherwood, PhD, RN, FAAN, ANEF,** is Professor Emerita at the University of North Carolina at Chapel Hill School of Nursing.

**Michelle Taylor Skipper, DNP, FNP-BC, NHDP-BC, FAANP,** is Director of the Adult-Gerontology and Family Nurse Practitioner specialties of the DNP program at the East Carolina University College of Nursing.

**Chandra L. Speight, PhD, RN, NP-C, CNE,** is Assistant Professor in the Department of Advanced Nursing Practice and Education at the East Carolina University College of Nursing.

**Allison Squires, PhD, RN, FAAN,** is Associate Professor and Director of the PhD program at the New York University Rory Meyers College of Nursing.

**Dennis A. Taylor, DNP, PhD, ACNP-BC, NEA-BC, FCCM,** is a Trauma Acute Care Nurse Practitioner and teaches in the Department of Academic Nursing at Wake Forest Baptist Health.

**Todd E. Tussing, DNP, RN, CENP, NEA-BC,** is Assistant Professor of Clinical Nursing at the Ohio State University College of Nursing.

**Gisela H. van Rensburg** is Professor at the University of South Africa.

**AnnMarie Lee Walton, PhD, MPH, RN, OCN, CHES, FAAN,** is Assistant Professor at the Duke University School of Nursing.

**Kefang Wang, PhD, RN, FAAN,** is Dean and Professor in the School of Nursing and Rehabilitation at Shandong University in China.

**Jean Watson, PhD, RN, AHN-BC, HSGAHN, FAAN, LL (AAN),** is Distinguished Professor and Founder/Director of the Watson Caring Science Institute in Colorado.

**Ena M. Williams, MBA/MSM, RN, CENP,** is Senior Vice President and Chief Nursing Officer at Yale New Haven Hospital.

**Kenichi Yamaguchi, PhD,** is Associate Professor at the Okinawa Prefectural College of Nursing in Japan.

# TABLE OF CONTENTS

# INTRODUCTION

This Learner Activities Workbook is designed to work with the textbook and follows a similar format. It includes reflective questions, narratives and discussion questions, activities, quizzes, and additional resources for the chapters. Learners can use the reflective questions and narratives to guide their reading, thinking, group discussions, or activities.

Like the textbook, this Learner Activities Workbook comprises five parts, which support nurse leaders' development in clinical practice or academic settings.

Below is a brief introduction of the five parts.

## PART I

The workbook presents leadership theories in organizations. There are four topics in this part, which are closely connected:

1. The evolution of leadership theories from ancient times to the present

2. Nursing as both discipline and profession shaped by the conditions and attributes of influential nurse leaders, historically relevant theoretical and philosophical perspectives, and paradigm shifts in healthcare

3. The influence of our knowledge of complex adaptive systems and the neuroscience of interactions on leadership development and implications for healthcare practices

4. Promotion of strengths-based leadership and positive leadership to help readers develop effective communication, conflict management, team building, and leadership skills

## PART II

Leadership's roles in creating healthy work environments are addressed. The four topics in this part support readers in establishing and promoting organizational culture and environments:

1. Ways to nurture a healthy and healing environment

2. Leadership's roles in promoting a resilient healthcare workforce

3. Leadership's opportunities in mitigating organizational trauma and supportive strategies from a Caring Science perspective

4. The role of planetary and environmental health in leading and enhancing human-universe relationships

# PART III

Four visionary leadership theories are applied in practice:

1.  Quantum Leadership and ways to integrate it into healthcare

2.  Using caring leadership and Caring Science to guide leadership practice

3.  Organizational strategies to promote exceptional patient experience through Compassionate Connected Care®

4.  The application of complexity theory to inform population and community health

# PART IV

The role of nurse leadership in collaboration, leading change, and innovation is presented:

1.  The importance of a unifying workforce to improve interprofessional collaboration and healthcare

2.  Reinforcing leadership's roles in collaboration for disaster preparedness and response

3.  The importance of collaboration and leading change at a global level

4.  Promoting research, quality, and evidence-informed practice

# PART V

The last part envisions the future of nurse leadership, defining wisdom leaders to inform personal and professional leadership development:

1.  Addressing diversity, equity, and inclusion (DEI) in academia and clinical settings and specific strategies to support BIPOC (Black, Indigenous, and people of color) nurse scholars

2.  Calling for nurses' and healthcare professionals' actions to advocate and get involved in policy change

3.  Healthcare leadership in social and political determinants of health

4.  Calling healthcare leaders to create a more connected world through an Ethic of Face and Belonging

With an emphasis on collaboration and partnerships, the textbook moves away from hierarchical forms of leadership to teach more engaged, open, equitable, inclusive, authentic, and caring leadership styles.

# 1

# THE EVOLUTION OF LEADERSHIP THEORIES

## REFLECTIVE QUESTIONS

1. How are Collaborative Leadership Theory and Complexity Leadership Theory similar? Different?

   _____

   _____

   _____

   _____

   _____

2. What leadership style might be most effective in a situation where immediate action is required? Why?

   _____

   _____

   _____

   _____

   _____

3. What are the four characteristics of transformational leaders?

a)

_____

_____

b)

_____

_____

c)

_____

_____

d)

_____

_____

4. According to Situational Leadership Theory, what factors determine the appropriate leadership style?

_____

_____

_____

_____

_____

5. Explain how Behavioral Leadership Theory is different from Trait Leadership Theory.

_____

_____

_____

_____

_____

# NARRATIVE

As a result of the COVID-19 pandemic, the healthcare industry has seen unprecedented disruption in its priorities, operations, and outcomes, challenging leadership and management to be much nimbler. Numerous changes in hospital patient population and services available have shifted to accommodate the influx of often seriously ill COVID-19 patients. At one hospital, all ancillary operations— outpatient surgery, hospice, wellness centers, community outreach, etc.— were closed and those staff either "rifted" or reassigned.

Your unit manager is preparing to move 25% of the nursing staff to help cover the growing COVID-19 units. At a staff meeting, the manager informs the group that this will be done by lottery, and anyone selected who refuses to go will be terminated.

Your friend who works on another unit informs you that his manager plans to poll all nurses to ascertain their thoughts and willingness to take on this new assignment and, if needed, confer individually with staff before making decisions.

Another colleague reported that her manager informed staff that it would be up to them to decide who would go to the COVID-19 units and that the group decision would be final.

# RESPONSE TO THE NARRATIVE

What management styles are these three managers exhibiting?

_____

_____

_____

_____

_____

_____

_____

# QUIZ QUESTIONS

1. Charismatic leaders are those who have a personality that is appealing, attractive, and influential to followers.

   a) True

   b) False

2. Trait theorists believe that leadership behaviors can be trained.

   a) True

   b) False

3. The Michigan Leadership Studies in the 1950s focused on supervisory behaviors and employee productivity and satisfaction.

   a) True

   b) False

4. The premise of contingency theories is that leadership success is situational.

   a) True

   b) False

5. Situational Leadership Theory contends that a static method of leading can be effective in varied circumstances.

   a) True

   b) False

6. Which of the following is not a characteristic of a servant leader?

   a) Listening

   b) Empathy

   c) Prudence

   d) Charisma

   e) Commitment

7. The Great Man Theory from the mid-late 1800s:

   a) Emerged from biographies of great men

   b) Asserted that great men are born, not made

   c) Described leadership as an immutable property gifted to exceptional people

   d) Ignited the interest in studying the qualities of leadership

   e) Believed one's leadership ability is innate

   f) All the above

8.  In the evolution of leadership theories, which theory came first:

    a) Path-Goal

    b) Trait Leadership Theory

    c) Behavioral Leadership Theory

    d) Transformational Leadership Theory

    e) Servant Leadership Theory

9.  Studies that examined the relationships between supervisors' behaviors and employees' productivity and satisfaction were:

    a) Ohio State University Studies

    b) Lewin's Behavioral Study

    c) Michigan Leadership Studies

    d) Blake and Mouton Managerial Leadership Grid Studies

10. Fiedler's Contingency Theory from the 1960s identified which two leadership styles? (choose all that apply)

    a) Task-oriented

    b) Directive

    c) Relation-oriented

    d) Decision-making

    e) Situational

# GLOBAL PERSPECTIVES ON THE EVOLUTION OF NURSING LEADERSHIP

## REFLECTIVE QUESTIONS

1. Identify a leader who influenced your own leadership journey. What stood out? What is an example of how this person has helped shape you as a nurse leader?

_____

_____

_____

_____

_____

_____

_____

2.  How did the global pandemic reveal your leadership capacity? What values and beliefs guided you?

_____

_____

_____

_____

_____

_____

3.  What leadership lessons will you take from your experiences during the COVID-19 pandemic? How will you look back five years or even 10 years from now to reflect on this stage of your leadership journey?

_____

_____

_____

_____

_____

_____

4.  How do leaders practice inclusive principles to help everyone feel they belong?

_____

_____

_____

_____

_____

_____

5.   When is a time that you felt excluded or ignored by your leader? How did you respond? What have you learned from this chapter to guide a future response?

_____

_____

_____

_____

_____

_____

_____

# NARRATIVE

Jennie notices that her post-operative patient has developed a urinary tract infection (UTI). She checks the chart and notes the number of days since the tubing had been changed, but no date is on the tubing. She sighs as she considers this lack of attentive nursing care. Jennie remembers that another nurse had also commented on the increase in UTIs. After confirming the standards of care for post-operative patients with an in-dwelling urinary catheter, Jennie found the other nurse and discussed her concern that the unit nurses may be slack in consistently following the evidence-based guidelines for catheter care. Should they speak up? Jennie has only been working on the unit for a year. She wonders if she has the leadership skills for bringing this to the unit council. Should she ask to lead a quality improvement project? She tries to recall leadership principles from her undergraduate program. While she feels inadequate, knowing that patients experienced unnecessary pain and suffering with a preventable UTI violates her values of quality, patient-centered care.

## RESPONSE TO THE NARRATIVE

- What steps should Jennie take next?

- What leadership principles can help guide her actions?

- What are ways novice leaders can become more confident in their leadership?

_____

_____

_____

_____

_____

_____

_____

## NARRATIVE

Jennie's supervisor, Sharon, the unit director, was new, having only worked on the unit two months. Her vision was to work towards a unit with high-quality standards, establish open communication among all team members, and develop trusting and respectful relationships with staff, patients, and other disciplines. As she reviewed the unit data, she noted the increase in UTIs. She wondered when the unit standards had been last reviewed and whether nurses were adhering to the standards. Should she create a CAUTI improvement team to take a deep dive into the issue to determine next steps? How would she be able to recruit staff to participate given they were short-staffed and everyone was still on edge due to increased pressures from the COVID-19 pandemic? She thought about the various stakeholders including physicians who may have an interest and share her passion to eliminate this preventable patient harm.

## RESPONSE TO THE NARRATIVE

- What steps should Sharon take next?

- What leadership principles can help guide her actions?

- What are ways she can establish an interprofessional team to investigate and design an improvement strategy?

- Although Jennie and Sharon are at different stages of their careers, each is facing new leadership challenges. What are similarities and differences in possible approaches for each of them?

_____

_____

_____

_____

_____

_____

_____

# QUIZ QUESTIONS

1.  What are ways for nurses to demonstrate leadership in influencing standards, guidelines, and policies that direct practice?

    a) Become informed of latest evidence on the topic of concern

    b) Apply evidence-based practice guidelines to distill best practices

    c) Enlist co-workers to join quality improvement team

    d) Collect case examples of how changing standards makes a difference

    e) All the above

2.  Characteristic of authentic leaders include:

    a) Ability to develop trust

    b) Ability to improve individual and team performance

    c) Value the input of others

    d) Truthfulness and openness

    e) All the above

3.  Leadership rooted in complexity science reveals the challenge of modern healthcare delivery with three primary constructs that include:

    a) Awakening, Connector, and Upholder

    b) Awakening, Builder, and Upholder

    c) Builder, Enhancer, and Sustainer

    d) Awakening, Enhancing, and Sustaining

4.  Three attributes of nurse leaders who embody caring competencies in order to build healthy work environments include:

    a) Communication, keeping commitments, and building and sustaining trust

    b) Communication, relationship management, and building and sustaining trust

    c) Building and sustaining trust, communication, and embracing diversity

    d) Relationship management, discovering potential, and keeping commitments

5.  Nursing leadership attributes that contribute to development and sustainability of a healthy work environment include:

    a) Developing collaboration

    b) Professional development

    c) Emotional intelligence

    d) Organizational climate

    e) All the above

6.  Describe how caring-based leadership is visible to others through the behaviors of the nurse leader.

    _____

    _____

    _____

    _____

    _____

7.  Discuss how global nursing leadership is helping to shape the future of healthcare.

    _____

    _____

    _____

    _____

    _____

8. Explore common threads of progressive models of nursing leadership.

_____

_____

_____

_____

_____

9. How would you apply relational coordination in leading interprofessional teams?

_____

_____

_____

_____

_____

10. What are differences between leadership and management?

_____

_____

_____

_____

_____

# **3**

# TRANSCENDING LEADERSHIP AND REDEFINING SUCCESS

## REFLECTIVE QUESTIONS

1. What type of environment cultivates leadership, and which theory is applicable to this type of environment?

   _____

   _____

   _____

   _____

   _____

2. A leader is no longer viewed as the captain of the ship but rather as a gardener. How does a gardener represent leadership?

   _____

   _____

   _____

   _____

   _____

3. What are the five social qualities used to determine the leader and her employees' reactions? What is the biological impact and response of these qualities on the body?

_____

_____

_____

_____

_____

4. How does Kouzes and Posner's five methods of leadership development affect complex adaptive systems and neuroscience?

_____

_____

_____

_____

_____

5. What facets must be considered for leadership development?

_____

_____

_____

_____

_____

# NARRATIVE

Jan has been a nurse for nine months; she works in a 30-bed intensive care unit. Typically, there are 17 nurses and one charge nurse on the unit during each shift, and the night shift charge nurse has been there for eight years; however, this night looks different. Tonight, there are only 14 nurses, 22 patients with the potential for eight admissions, and Jan was pulled to the charge nurse position with the possibility of having her own patient(s), depending on the number of admissions and the acuity of the patients. Jan was shifted to the charge role because she has the most experience on nights compared to the other nursing staff. The other nursing staff consists of four nurses who have six months of experience, and the others are newly off orientation. Jan is nervous about being the charge nurse for the night because she fears her experience is not enough to lead the team, and she has not had an orientation to the role. The night shift team senses her nervousness and anxiety.

# RESPONSE TO THE NARRATIVE

1.  Five social qualities determine the leader and the employee's reactions: status, certainty, autonomy, relatedness, and fairness. How do these qualities affect both Jan and the team?

    _____

    _____

    _____

    _____

    _____

    _____

2.  What elements of a complex adaptive system influences this unit and this situation?

    _____

    _____

    _____

    _____

    _____

    _____

3.  Based on neuroleadership, what steps can be taken to improve the situation and the overall reactions of Jan and the team?

_____

_____

_____

_____

_____

_____

4.  What steps can be taken to ensure those who are shifted into leadership roles are well equipped and well trained for success?

_____

_____

_____

_____

_____

_____

_____

_____

# QUIZ QUESTIONS

1. What things do the new models of leadership development incorporate? (select all that apply)

    a) Knowledge from both professional experience and evidence-based

    b) Recognizing the impact of complex adaptive systems on the organization

    c) Incorporating the neuroscience of interpersonal relationships among leaders and their followers

    d) Employing Sustainable Development Goals (SDGs) in leadership development and actions

2. A good leader recognizes the extent of their influence and how change occurs in a non-linear or unpredictable system.

    a) True

    b) False

3. Experienced behavior is a feature of complex adaptive systems represented by constant innovation and creativity.

    a) True

    b) False

4. What are the key elements of complex adaptive systems (CAS) for leaders to understand?

    a) Linearity and unpredictability

    b) Nonlinearity and unpredictability

    c) Linearity and predictability

    d) Nonlinearity and predictability

5. Implications of leadership include which of the following? (select all that apply)

    a) Value individuality versus the interprofessional approach

    b) Emphasize the importance of a learning environment where things are tried and some work and some do not; expecting and welcoming failure leads to a learning environment

    c) Discourage self-organization

    d) Recognize different perspectives as a good thing and that a healthy level of conflict promotes progress

6. What are the five reactions of the SCARF model?

    a) Status, Change, Autonomy, Relatedness, and Fairness

    b) Status, Certainty, Autonomy, Relatedness, and Fairness

    c) Status, Change, Adaptability, Relatedness, and Fairness

    d) Status, Certainty, Autonomy, Responsibility, and Fairness

7. Five social qualities were found to determine the leader and the employees' reactions. One social quality affecting reaction is status. Status can be beneficial or threatening. A benefit of status is longevity while a threat is stress.

    a) True

    b) False

8. Five social qualities were found to determine the leader and the employees' reactions. One social quality affecting reaction is fairness. Fairness can be beneficial or threatening. A benefit of fairness is being calm while a threat is being disengaged.

    a) True

    b) False

9. Navigating the human psyche requires leaders to "speak" to which of the following functions in order to achieve success? (select all that apply)

    a) Thinking

    b) Feeling

    c) Learning

    d) Behaving

10. There is evidence from psychology and organizational behavior that a leader's mental and emotional state will be reflected by their followers.

    a) True

    b) False

# 4

# DEVELOPING EFFECTIVE LEADERSHIP SKILLS AND CAPACITY

## REFLECTIVE QUESTIONS

1. What are factors critical to the development of strengths-based leadership for nurse leaders?

_____

_____

_____

_____

_____

_____

_____

2.  Please describe the sources of power in organizations.

_____

_____

_____

_____

_____

_____

3.  What are the key components of leadership's effective communication?

_____

_____

_____

_____

_____

_____

4.  Please describe the five modes to solve conflicts.

_____

_____

_____

_____

_____

_____

5. What is positive leadership?

_____

_____

_____

_____

_____

_____

_____

# NARRATIVE

One Monday morning, when Megan, the nurse manager of a surgical unit, stepped into the unit, she saw that everyone was busy. She noticed that the unit code cart was parked outside Room 1, and the code team was in the room. She was informed that a new nurse administered the wrong dose of medicine to the patient in Room 1. The patient was transferred to the ICU after the code. Once things had calmed down, Megan called the nurse to her office and asked, "What happened?" The nurse said, "I was very busy with my patients and heard other nurses talking about me. I kept thinking about what they had said about me. I was upset. I was distracted and pulled the wrong dose of medicine." Megan could tell the nurse felt terrible, and then she mumbled, "I want them to like me. I should not be distracted by them." Megan did not understand what the nurse meant and questioned the nurse, "What are you talking about?"

In the following few days, the nurse called out sick. A few weeks later, the nurse submitted her resignation letter to Megan and left the unit. A few other nurses also left the unit consecutively. Megan started to realize the necessity to evaluate the unit's work environment. She recognized a need for a change in culture in her unit.

# RESPONSE TO THE NARRATIVE

What should the nurse manager, Megan, do in response to her unit's situation? Megan starts the change from the following aspects:

_____

_____

_____

_____

_____

_____

_____

# QUIZ QUESTIONS

1.  The basis of strengths-based leadership is _____.

    a) Identifying and minimizing weaknesses

    b) Working with an executive coach

    c) Maximizing identified strengths

    d) Completing a course on strengths in leadership

2.  Self-development based on strengths-based leadership includes all the following except: _____.

    a) Ignoring blind spots, as they are a weakness

    b) Working with a peer to obtain feedback on interactions

    c) Reflection on what went well

    d) Lifelong learning

3.  Organizational politics are not important if you work hard and do a good job.

    a) True

    b) False

4.  Involvement in Big "P" politics involves the following except_____:

    a) Volunteering for the legislative committee of a professional organization

    b) Working on a political campaign

    c) Writing legislators regarding proposed healthcare legislation

    d) Reading the information sent out by professional organizations and voting

5.  Development of a power base is important in organizations and may be enhanced by _____.

    a) Developing relationships with influential leaders

    b) Displaying confidence and competence in an area of importance

    c) Being conscientious in completing all tasks

    d) All the above

    e) a & b only

6.  Power generated by association with another is _____.

    a) Expert power

    b) Referent power

    c) Coercive power

    d) Influence power

7.  All the following are examples of human capital except _____.

    a) Position capital

    b) Political capital

    c) Social capital

    d) Intellectual capital

8.  A communication model that incorporates sender, receiver, message, life experiences, culture, values, and education is called _____.

    a) Linear Model

    b) Interactional Model

    c) Teleport Model

    d) Systems Model

9.  All the following are key areas leaders should consider when drafting a message except_____.

    a) Message (what needs to be conveyed)

    b) Method of message (e.g., in person, written, etc.)

    c) Time of message

    d) Teleport model

10. In 2001, the American Association of Critical-Care Nurses began promoting a framework called _____ to combat horizontal violence in the workplace.

    a) Healthy Work Environment

    b) Transactional Model

    c) COPE Model

    d) SWOT Analysis

11.   An important element of a team's cohesion is _____.

   a) Diversity

   b) Trust

   c) Location

   d) Number of members

12.   One major change in team dynamics due to the COVID-19 pandemic is _____.

   a) Dress code

   b) Moving to a virtual format

   c) Time of meetings

   d) Number of members

13.   Nursing leaders mentoring virtual teams must do all the following except:

   a) Make sure policies and procedures support the team

   b) Work with information technology to secure the most advanced technology possible

   c) Check in with team members regularly for any needs

   d) Use emojis and encoding emotions or sound effects in message language extensively

14.   Recognizing the importance "influence" has on leadership/member interactions, which document has "influence" embedded into a competency?

   a) American Association of Critical-Care Nurses Healthy Work Environment

   b) American Organization of Nursing Leadership Nurse Executive Competencies

   c) Institute of Medicine's To Err Is Human

   d) United States government's Healthy People 2030

15.   Leadership models can help leaders focus and practice on skills to be more effective. Which of the following is an example of a leadership model a new nurse leader can utilize in practice?

   a) The Human-Centered Leadership Model

   b) Krebs Cycle Model

   c) ARC Framework (Competency, Regulation, Attachment)

   d) The IOWA Model

# 5

# NURTURING HEALTHY AND HEALING WORK ENVIRONMENTS

## REFLECTIVE QUESTIONS

1. Reflect on theoretical nursing knowledge and your values and strengths as a nurse. How are they visible and invisible in your role as a nurse leader?

_____

_____

_____

_____

_____

_____

_____

2.  What intentional healing practices do you use that demonstrate care for yourself? For others?

_____

_____

_____

_____

_____

_____

_____

3.  How do you currently use reflective practice in your personal and professional life? What more can you do? Why does it matter?

_____

_____

_____

_____

_____

_____

_____

4.  Describe the landscape of your current healthcare environment. What is the most important step you can take, as a leader, to integrate healing practices into the environment?

_____

_____

_____

_____

_____

_____

5.  How does your well-being influence you and your role as a nurse leader who develops and applies nursing knowledge?

_____

_____

_____

_____

_____

_____

_____

# NARRATIVE

You are a nurse manager on an inpatient medical-surgical unit and have been in your position for two years. While the clinical environment is beginning to settle into a new normal after COVID-19, you have lost a number of staff and experienced changes at the bedside at a more rapid pace than before. At the same time, the organization is requesting you start a number of new quality and safety initiatives, and you are faced with competing priorities. In addition to a stressful environment, you have very little time to yourself or to check in with staff due to being in meetings all day long. You get home to receive a call that the unit is short-staffed with three nurses for 24 patients. You have a six-month-old baby at home and want to spend time with your family but feel guilty leaving your nurses short-staffed. These types of situations are occurring more and more frequently at work.

# RESPONSE TO THE NARRATIVE

What intentional practices will help you navigate care for yourself and others and influence the organization to create a more healing environment?

_____

_____

_____

_____

_____

_____

_____

_____

_____

# QUIZ QUESTIONS

1.  Attending to the healing process is ultimately what will result in a healthy and healing work environment.

    a) True

    b) False

2.  Which of the following are elements of a healthy work environment?

    a) Fosters self-care and well-being

    b) Safe

    c) Empowering

    d) Evidence-based practice education

    e) All the above

3.  It is the responsibility of the nurse to develop a healthy work environment.

    a) True

    b) False

4.  Which theorist highlights the importance of being present when interacting with others, acknowledging others' viewpoints, and unfolding meaning with presence to enhance the quality of work-life both for themselves and for others?

    a) Watson

    b) Parse

    c) Palmer

    d) Watkins

5.  How might one utilize and implement nursing theory and research to create healthy work environments?

    a) Theory and research provide a framework that guides inquiry.

    b) Theories should be implemented to enhance mindfulness.

    c) Testing theories and research in an organization to prove a healthy work environment.

    d) None of the above.

6.  Self-care is an iterative process.

    a) True

    b) False

7.  Which of the following are characterized as intentional individual self-care practices?

    a) Being authentic and true to oneself

    b) Mindfulness

    c) Gratitude

    d) Self-awareness

    e) Reflective practice

    f) All the above

8.  What is the definition of mindfulness?

    a) Focusing on the future

    b) Sitting in silence

    c) Being present in the current moment without judgment

    d) Praying

9.  How does one reach a state of being rather than doing in the profession of nursing?

> a) Practicing mindfulness
>
> b) Any intentional practice that connects mind, body, and spirit while staying in the present
>
> c) Authentically connecting with others and the environment
>
> d) All the above

10. What characteristics assist in authentic leadership and promote a healthy work environment? (choose all that apply)

> a) Knowing oneself, bringing values to work, and creating an empowering environment for others to share their perspectives
>
> b) Representing the values of the organization, even at the risk of misalignment with your values
>
> c) Being an effective communicator
>
> d) Acting as an advocate for resources for staff

# 6

# LEADERSHIP ROLES IN PROMOTING A RESILIENT WORKFORCE

## REFLECTIVE QUESTIONS

1. Describe the effects that compassion fatigue can have on caregivers, patients, and organizations.

   _____

   _____

   _____

   _____

   _____

2. Discuss why leadership is important to resiliency when self-care is a personal practice/decision.

   _____

   _____

   _____

   _____

3.   List three attributes of a leader who is focused on care provider resiliency.

a)

_____

_____

b)

_____

_____

c)

_____

_____

4.   Describe the difference in healthcare providers' experience when working on a unit that prioritizes support, resiliency, and recovery vs. a unit that does not.

_____

_____

_____

_____

_____

5.   What are some offerings that an organization can prioritize to help build a resiliency culture in healthcare?

_____

_____

_____

_____

_____

# NARRATIVE

Behavioral Health Specialists are responsible for direct patient care and safety, including supervision and management of children and adolescents who may be experiencing a psychiatric crisis. Behavioral Health Specialists work in diverse environments, including inpatient psychiatric units, partial hospitalization or day treatment programs, and medical floors. One Behavioral Health Specialist named Neena, working in the psychiatric department of a large children's hospital, participated in a 12-week workshop designed to create community and develop resilience using artmaking. This workshop was facilitated by an art therapist, using a sequential curriculum within a peer-reviewed research protocol. Each week, Neena attended the group, looking forward to the chance to focus on herself, her creativity, and new relationships with other providers with similar self-care goals. Neena practiced different therapeutic skills and art-making techniques, building her confidence as well as her ability to be vulnerable. On the seventh week, she was asked to visually represent an especially challenging day at work, one that she may not be able to forget. Neena created an image of the day she was physically assaulted by a patient in distress. The image included red prison bars, representing her feeling of being trapped in the situation, and a red pool of blood at the bottom, which was her own. The image itself brought Neena to tears as she shared it with the group, recounting the story that she had not shared with anyone since it happened 12 weeks prior.

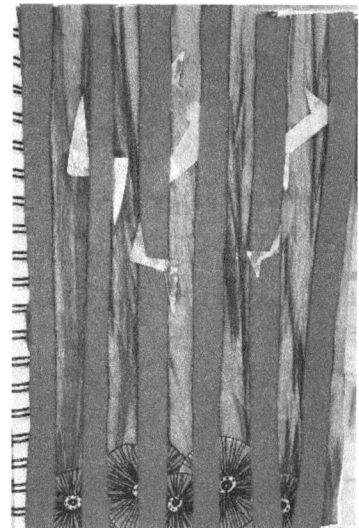

Original art by Neena, Behavioral Health Specialist

The group witnessed her courage and vulnerability in this process, offering her words of support and understanding. Neena left that day exhausted but relieved to have let this trauma pour out of her onto paper. She came back the following week feeling refreshed and rejuvenated, with new purpose and perspective on her professional worth.

In the last few weeks of the group, participants were asked to share artwork and writing for a collaborative artwork, with the goal of sharing their voices beyond the intimate setting of the group. Neena wrote the following to accompany another artwork she had created, depicting another intense day:

Behind the mask, tears are streaming down my face and my adrenaline is pumping harder than it has in my entire life. I can hear my own heartbeat, and the pounding in my ears is terrifying. One of my coworkers starts counting down from 3, and I know that once we get to 1, we're releasing our grip on the door handle and entering our patient's room to put them into a supine hold. This step, while traumatic for both the patient and for staff, is necessary at this moment to maintain the safety of our patient and everyone else on our unit. Knowing that doesn't make it any easier. Once we get to 1, I have to face the reality that I may witness one or more of my coworkers getting hurt. I have to accept that I may no longer have control and could get hurt myself. I have to be the most aware and present I have ever been to ensure our patient remains safe. 3, 2, 1. I take a deep breath, and I step forward.

Behind the mask, I am a Behavioral Health Specialist working on a psychiatric unit during a global pandemic. Sometimes my job is rewarding beyond what I could ever imagine. Feeling the impact we have on our patients and witnessing the changes they can make is amazing. At the same time, I have left work countless times crying, dehydrated, bruised, bleeding, or covered in bodily fluids. I've continually surprised myself with my ability to step up to the plate, but being the holder of someone else's pain and trauma is never easy and always weighs on you. Something I've taken away from our art group is that this is a shared sentiment among healthcare workers, yet we never back down. We continue to show up, day in and day out, for our patients and for our coworkers. We find ways to build resilience and we lean on each other. We step up to the plate in hard or scary situations, and that makes us brave. Throughout this group experience and my reflections on the past year of working in healthcare during a pandemic, I've been reminded that despite everything, hope and courage still persist.

*Original art by Neena, Behavioral Health Specialist*

# RESPONSE TO THE NARRATIVE

After reading through the experience of the healthcare provider in the narrative, what can you appreciate about a resiliency approach that includes different creative modalities to help staff process their trauma and reconnect to their individual purpose?

_____

_____

_____

_____

_____

_____

_____

_____

_____

# QUIZ QUESTIONS

1. What leadership styles are complementary with promoting resiliency in healthcare providers?

     a) Transformational

     b) Servant

     c) Authentic

     d) All the above

2. Emotional labor measures not only the quantity of care provided but also considers the quality of the experiences of care.

     a) True

     b) False

3. What are important factors for leaders to pay attention to regarding how their team members recover from stress? (choose all that apply)

     a) Are they on call regardless of the time of day?

     b) As a leader I should not get involved in such personal practices.

     c) Do they answer emails even when they are on vacation?

     d) None of the above.

4. Compassion fatigue not only considers the inability to care for patients but also the distress it has on the care provider themselves.

     a) True

     b) False

5. Arrange the following answers in the correct order for the team-based approach to build resiliency within a department.

     a) Create a road map for action

     b) Identify core values of each team member

     c) List action items to align with each value

     d) Prioritize values among the entire team

6. If I don't see myself as an artist, then using art to process stress won't work.

     a) True

     b) False

7. What do Caring Science workshops give the participants?

   a) A time to reconnect to purpose

   b) A way to practice loving-kindness for self and others

   c) A pause to honor the unique role caregivers have in healthcare

   d) A time to be surrounded and supported by peers who understand your experiences

   e) All the above

8. Team members will see their leader as weak if they show their own vulnerabilities and talk about what they need to build resiliency.

   a) True

   b) False

9. One of the most important starting points for organizations to begin building a resilient workforce is to:

   a) Hire people who do not seem to be affected by stress

   b) Remind care providers that they should care for themselves outside of work

   c) Recognize emotional labor as part of choosing to become a care provider and prioritize recovery as part of the work

   d) Set up a yoga program after work hours

10. Practicing self-care and fostering resilience are the least important priorities to consider as a healthcare provider.

    a) True

    b) False

# 7

# LEADERSHIP ROLES IN MITIGATING ORGANIZATIONAL TRAUMA

## REFLECTIVE QUESTIONS

1.  Consider an experience that made you feel traumatized at your workplace. What was the situation? What happened to you? How would you describe (a) the event, (b) the experience, (c) the effects of the workplace trauma?

_____

_____

_____

_____

_____

_____

_____

2.  Could you describe the strategies that leaders can use to help you heal from that trauma?

_____

_____

_____

_____

_____

_____

_____

3.  How do you as a nurse leader impact the organization and help it heal and remain a healing organization?

_____

_____

_____

_____

_____

_____

_____

4.  What are your suggestions for organizational leadership teams to promote a caring-healing environment?

_____

_____

_____

_____

_____

_____

5.  Describe ways to enhance organizational post-traumatic growth.

_____

_____

_____

_____

_____

_____

_____

# NARRATIVE

Jameson Hospital is a 530-bed acute care hospital. The critical care unit has 12 beds and is typically 90% occupied. Typically, there are six nurses on each shift. On a Thursday night, the unit had 12 patients, and one of the night shift nurses had called in, leaving five nurses on duty to work 7 pm to 7 am. During the shift, Nancy grabbed some medication and cross-checked it with Sarah. Nancy went into room 12 and administered the medication; within minutes the patient went into V-fib. A code was called and during the middle of resuscitation, Nancy realized she had pulled the wrong dosage of the medication resulting in the patient arresting. Nancy immediately told the physician running the code hoping that the information would help save the patient. The patient died. The family was informed of the death. However, no one informed the family of the cause of the death. The organization reported both Nancy and Sarah to the Board of Nursing, resulting in Nancy losing her license and Sarah being placed on probation. The nursing staff slowly became aware of what had happened as both nurses were friends with other nurses in the unit and everyone was heartsick over the loss of two critical care nurses, and the short staffing that everyone felt played into the outcome. The hospital administration held a staff meeting telling everyone to not discuss the case. Each week that passed, the nursing staff sunk deeper into depression. The nurse who had called out sick that night ended up resigning after four weeks, unable to take the side glances; it seemed everyone was wondering if she had worked her shift, would this have happened? Even those nurses who worked on the night shift eventually resigned over the course of four months.

# RESPONSE TO THE NARRATIVE

1.  Describe how organizational trauma evolved in this case.

_____

_____

_____

_____

_____

_____

_____

_____

_____

_____

2.  Discuss the cumulative impacts of organizational trauma in this scenario.

_____

_____

_____

_____

_____

3.  Describe ways of using caring consciousness and actions to promote organizational caring-healing when trauma occurs.

_____

_____

_____

_____

_____

4.  Explain how the Sanctuary Model could be utilized as a viable approach in this case.

_____

_____

_____

_____

_____

# QUIZ QUESTIONS

1.  Unrecognized wounding is a pattern of trauma in organizations. Which of the following is an example of unrecognized wounding?

    a) An African American nurse is met with workplace violence by a patient's family members as they mutter racial slurs under their breath; her reporting of the event is minimized.

    b) A school of nursing and a community hospital are at odds over an adverse event attributed to a student nurse.

    c) Rumors about working conditions and constant nurse turnover cause a hospital to become even more short-staffed.

    d) Gossiping, incivility, and interpersonal conflicts become the norm for organizational communication.

2. What would be an appropriate comment made by a trauma-informed supervisor?

   a) "In looking at your performance, I need to ask, what is wrong with you?"

   b) "Let me tell you about how badly stressed out I was! I almost couldn't function. I ended up getting fired."

   c) "I want to encourage you to reset that critical voice inside you and compare it to your actual performance."

   d) "We really need to improve on certain things. You just seem 'out of it' half the time. Care to tell me about it?"

3. In praxis of embracing the organization for healing, forgiveness is described. Which of the following statements best captures forgiveness within the organization?

   a) Transparency in organizational communications will allow employees to understand how decisions are made.

   b) The authentic leader speaks to optimism and energy, reminding employees of the mission of the organization.

   c) The nurse manager demonstrates presence, empathy, and benevolence toward nurses who have experienced trauma.

   d) Employees are encouraged to release the past and move forward, thereby avoiding the toxicity that can arise from holding onto old grudges and mistakes.

4. Which of the following does *not* exemplify "resisting re-traumatization" in organizations?

   a) Organizational leaders revise procedures for patient assessment to include assessment of past traumatic events using trauma-informed language.

   b) Organizational leaders plan a retreat for upper managers to ensure optimal coding is in place for third party payor reimbursement.

   c) A system-wide orientation is implemented to cover basic principles of trauma-informed practices.

   d) Policies and procedures for debriefing after a workplace violence event are reviewed to ensure trauma-informed practices.

5.  Appreciative Inquiry (AI) is a way of bridging how organizations heal from trauma and envision a new, strengths-based approach. When comparing an organizational trauma-informed approach with AI, which of the following is true?

   a) Appreciative Inquiry is a strengths-based approach, while a trauma-informed approach concentrates on individual deficits.

   b) Appreciative Inquiry is a strengths-based approach, while a trauma-informed approach is one of knowledge- and skills-based strategies to process and heal from individual and collective trauma.

   c) Appreciative Inquiry and trauma-informed approaches are both deficit-based approaches.

   d) Appreciative Inquiry addresses the individual, while a trauma-informed approach is about maximizing organizational resources.

# ADDITIONAL RESOURCES: SELECTED WEBSITES

## AMERICAN ASSOCIATION OF COLLEGES OF NURSING

https://www.aacnnursing.org/

The American Association of Colleges of Nursing (AACN) is the national voice for academic nursing. AACN works to establish quality standards for nursing education, assists schools in implementing those standards, influences the nursing profession to improve healthcare, and promotes public support for professional nursing education, research, and practice.

## AMERICAN NURSES ASSOCIATION

https://www.nursingworld.org/

American Nurses Association (ANA) has been championing the interests of registered nurses for more than 100 years. It advocates for nurses, supporting nurses at all career stages.

# HEALTHCARE LEADERSHIP IN PLANETARY AND ENVIRONMENTAL HEALTH

## REFLECTIVE QUESTIONS

1. Why might it be helpful to seek out nature when considering an important work challenge, life question, or career choice?

_____

_____

_____

_____

_____

2.  As nurse leaders, why is it important to consider how we, as a society, address the social determinants of health?

_____

_____

_____

_____

_____

3.  How did we become a society so fraught with loneliness and anxiety, and how is that contributing to health risks? What can we do about this?

_____

_____

_____

_____

_____

4.  How might national nursing organizations begin to advocate for positive changes regarding the social determinants of health, and why does that really require collective action?

_____

_____

_____

_____

_____

5.  What does the more beautiful world our hearts know is possible look like? Think expansively. Paint it as clearly as possible.

_____

_____

_____

_____

_____

# GROUP ACTIVITY PHASE ONE

In your group, take turns identifying the "systems" that make up our communities, and describe what works and doesn't work regarding these systems and what are sometimes the unintended consequences of the systems. Draw the system(s) as directed by the facilitator.

1.  What are the positive and negative effects of this system?

_____

_____

_____

_____

_____

2.  What are the health-promoting aspects of this system and what are not?

    _____

    _____

    _____

    _____

    _____

    _____

    _____

# GROUP ACTIVITY PHASE TWO

After working with the system and discussing it, see if your group can think of another system to draw. Repeat the process from Phase One.

# QUIZ QUESTIONS

1.  As outlined by Brian Mertins, who is involved in nature mentoring, which of the following can be learned in nature:

    a) Presence and Awareness

    b) Gratitude and Appreciation

    c) Relationships and Emotional Intelligence

    d) All the above

2.  According to the World Health Organization, what percentage of global diseases are attributed to the social determinants of health?

    a) 10–25%

    b) 30–55%

    c) 60–80%

    d) 90%

3.  The healthcare system is currently configured to address the social determinants of health.

    a) True

    b) False

4.  What "ailment" did US Surgeon General Vivek Murthy observe to be contributing to increased mortality as much as smoking or obesity?

    a) Cancer

    b) Food insecurity

    c) Loneliness

    d) Autoimmune diseases

5.  According to a Cigna study, more teens are feeling more socially isolated than ever before.

    a) True

    b) False

6.  Why are the ailments noted in this chapter important for nursing leaders to know and acknowledge?

_____

_____

_____

_____

_____

7.  Planetary health is a new conceptual framework that recognizes that humans should have dominion over the natural world.

    a) True

    b) False

8.  In addition to the healthcare system, what other systems should nursing leaders understand when addressing the complex causes of disease?

    a) Economic

    b) Political

    c) Ecological

    d) All the above

9. Reframing our message from what we are against to what we are for will allow us to develop more hopeful messages.

     a) True

     b) False

10. The use of the Mother Tree in this chapter is helpful in considering some of the basic but profound shifts that may be necessary to achieve human and planetary health. What are some of the shifts that you think are the most important right now?

_____

_____

_____

_____

_____

# QUANTUM CARING LEADERSHIP: A NEW ONTOLOGY INTO PRACTICE

## REFLECTIVE QUESTIONS

1. In light of your experience and the learning from this chapter, how do you integrate the Caritas Processes into practice including care for self, others, and organization/community?

_____

_____

_____

_____

_____

_____

_____

2.  How is unitary consciousness visible in your role as a nurse leader? What more can you do?

_____

_____

_____

_____

_____

_____

_____

3.  What does Quantum Caring Leadership mean to you?

_____

_____

_____

_____

_____

_____

_____

4.  How can the principles of Quantum Caring Leadership be utilized to sustain humanity?

_____

_____

_____

_____

_____

_____

_____

5.   Why does embracing a unitary quantum caring worldview matter?

_____

_____

_____

_____

_____

_____

_____

# NARRATIVE

An invitation to present to the regional quality council of a large healthcare system was extended to a Chief Nurse Executive (CNE), the direct result of notable and sustained improvements in quality outcomes, operational performance, and service metrics over a two-year period.

In sharing the team's story, the CNE identified that despite dutifully implementing the same system-wide initiatives and best practices supported by detailed playbooks, checklists, and service scripts, their hospital's scorecard remained among the lowest in the region. Following extended leadership gaps and turnover, the new and current nurse executive assessed the landscape, identified a unique and disruptive opportunity, and proposed a different approach to address performance gaps that involved the integration of established Caring Science Theory and emerging Quantum Leadership principles. The leadership and clinical teams were engaged and subsequently espoused their support during open leader forums, enthusiastically embracing the vision to actively transform their culture through Quantum Caring Leadership (QCL) principles, evidence, and informed moral action.

The leadership message and commitment were that this hospital or community of leaders and care teams would begin a journey to consciously lead and act through human connections and authentic caring relationships. Conventional leadership approaches had previously focused on controlling processes, competency, metrics, and compliance. They were fostering trust, and shifting the culture required education, mentoring, coaching, and role modeling that was both ubiquitous and aligned with QCL. Teams had to discover new ways of being and becoming together, unlearning divisive or separatist thinking and developing evolved practices that were more congruent with Quantum Caring Leadership. The focus was on supporting the ongoing development of confident, caring clinicians and leaders committed to establishing an authentic, caring, compassionate, and healing culture. Learning forums were conducted regularly to model appreciative dialogue and discover the shared meaning behind new or emerging initiatives. Change was no longer something to fear or resist but increasingly perceived as an opportunity to learn, grow, adapt, and improve care together. Clinicians were engaged every step of the way and soon adopted a credo, "Nothing about us, without us!" to represent their commitment to full engagement. In addition to authentic dialogue and intentional inclusion, decisions were no longer made in an office but encouraged and supported to be made as close to the point of care as possible. Experiential learning events on QCL, Caring Science integration, and the 10 Caritas Processes helped guide leader and care team commitments to self-care, resilience, connectedness, caring moments, and healing environments. Growing evidence of intentionality, presence, connectedness, and authentic caring connections was best reflected in narratives. Inviting and celebrating caring moments prior to meetings and in shift huddles/cuddles helped infuse a steady sense of joy and meaning in the collective work.

In closure, the CNE reinforced that hospital leaders have continually evolved and come to value their role as navigators, translators, and champions of a harmonizing QCL message that unites teams under a common vision in order to achieve uncommon results. Their commitment to relationships and connectedness helped engender trust, and through consistent QCL practices, they have nurtured ongoing growth, quality, success, and the ability for patients, individuals, teams, and the organization to flourish together. Empowered through QCL practices, care teams are increasingly aware, fully engaged, and owning their practice, which has been observed to be a liberating, organic, transformative, renewable, and an indispensable source of continued success and sustained performance as a caring community.

# ACTIVITY

In pairs or small groups, create a list of Quantum Caring Leadership (QCL) characteristics identified in the case study. Referring to the list of QCL characteristics, share a leadership experience with your group where QCL characteristics were either clearly evident or notably absent. Discuss the potential impact of sustained congruence between theory and leadership practices (QCL) on patient care, the nursing workforce, and organizational performance.

---

## BEING, BECOMING, AND DOING AS A QCL

**BEING:** The quantum caring leader exists at the highly complex and continually evolving intersections of the organization. It is here that the self-aware and conscious leader must assess, sort, translate, interpret, predict, and ultimately make decisions.

**BECOMING:** Engagement is a dynamic, relationship-centric journey to intentionally harmonize quantum caring leader and team alignment through a shared commitment to a common mission, vision, and congruent set of values.

**DOING:** Living out QCL requires authentic presence, role modeling, coaching, and ongoing evaluation to nurture a continuously evolving and thriving quantum caring community.

# RESPONSE TO THE ACTIVITY

Use the space below to reflect on the activity.

_____

_____

_____

_____

_____

_____

_____

_____

_____

_____

# QUIZ QUESTIONS

1. Which statement best describes a unitary worldview?

     a) Relationships require time.

     b) Environment is controlled.

     c) Everything is connected.

     d) Focus is service-oriented.

2. Separatist views found in leadership may include all the following except:

     a) Top-down decision making

     b) Focus on control

     c) Reductionist processes

     d) Change as a dynamic

3. Quantum worldview parallels the growing commitment of nursing scholars to unitary thinking for nursing phenomena.

     a) True

     b) False

4.  Second quantum concepts of "non-locality" and "non-local consciousness" are best defined as:

    a) Both universe and communication can be non-local.

    b) Consciousness is not confined to the brain.

    c) Both a & b.

    d) None of the above.

5.  Healthcare leadership today is generally more unitary and evolved than Newtonian separatist or otherwise outdated transactional leadership principles.

    a) True

    b) False

6.  Caring Science Theory seeks to sustain human caring-healing and love, through:

    a) Knowledgeable and compassionate service to humankind

    b) Enhanced value for nursing care through evidence and metrics

    c) Caritas Processes that offer a checklist for creating caring relationships

    d) Advanced service-oriented models with theory-guided caring moments

7.  New patterns of Quantum Caring Leadership principles offer directions for fixing broken systems through improved caregiver engagement and accountability.

    a) True

    b) False

8.  The congruence that unites quantum and caring leadership helps advance:

    a) Newtonian and transactional leadership tactics

    b) Distinct disciplinary foundations for new leadership practices and principles

    c) Innovative perspectives to manage operational efficiency and performance

    d) Established healthcare leadership theory, knowledge, and practices

9.  An evolved Quantum Caring Leadership model invites new leadership thinking, critique, and consciousness for all healthcare leadership.

    a) True

    b) False

10. As Caring Science knowledge evolves toward the integration of "second quantum revolution" science, it aligns to Quantum Leadership ethics and principles that support a nursing specific leadership model.

    a) True

    b) False

# CARING SCIENCE-INFORMED LEADERSHIP

## REFLECTIVE QUESTIONS

1. How is Caritas Leadership visible in your practice? What more can you do?

_____

_____

_____

_____

_____

_____

_____

2.  What distinguishes Caritas/Caring Science–informed leadership from conventional patterns of leadership?

_____

_____

_____

_____

_____

_____

_____

3.  How do Caritas leaders create a caring, healing environment?

_____

_____

_____

_____

_____

_____

_____

4.  Why is it essential for an academic Caritas leader to trust that people are able?

_____

_____

_____

_____

_____

_____

_____

5.   How would you describe Caritas leaders in the academy?

_____

_____

_____

_____

_____

_____

_____

# ACTIVITY

Reflect on your individual, current nursing leadership experiences and ways you are integrating and/or how you can begin to integrate Caring Science–informed leadership practices. In the space below, explore some experiences and goals you can share in a group activity.

_____

_____

_____

_____

_____

_____

_____

_____

_____

_____

Follow up:  Choose one Caritas Leadership practice to integrate and share your goal with your group. In the space below, identify the practice, explain how you will integrate it, and how you can share your goal in a follow-up group activity:

_____

_____

_____

_____

_____

_____

_____

_____

_____

_____

# QUIZ QUESTIONS

1.  Caritas leaders consider caring as a moral imperative to act ethically and justly.

      a) True

      b) False

2.  Caring Leadership is a way of being, knowing, and doing that facilitates human flourishing for leaders, staff, students, and their organizations.

      a) True

      b) False

3.  A caring, healing environment is experienced by nurse leaders as "the disconnected, illiterate unconscious actions and practices from a dehumanizing organization."

      a) True

      b) False

4.  Caritas leaders consider all actors' perceptions and past experiences and their meanings to collaboratively engage and commit to the leader's vision regarding the transformation's insight.

    a) True

    b) False

5.  Caritas leaders were invited to know themselves and others as caring persons to "seek new solutions" to challenges, difficulties, and problems from a Caring Science perspective.

    a) True

    b) False

6.  The ontology of Caritas Leadership literacy begins and ends with self and invites leaders to:

    a) Form (versus deform)

    b) Guide the human creative spirit, away from the outer patterned, non-relational system-cultures (dyspraxis)

    c) Reconstruct, drawing upon inner subjective, creative life force of self/other in relation—co-creating Caritas ontological eupraxis as foundation for Caring Science Leadership

    d) All the above

7.  Caritas leaders in acute care settings engage their hearts by engaging in which of these practices?

    a) Caring hiring practices, annual performance evaluations, and self-care practice interventions

    b) Coaching and mentoring relationships and strategic goal integration

    c) Self-care micro practices, authentic presence, and mindful listening

    d) Providing comfort measures, psychological safety, privacy, and aesthetic surroundings

8.  Which Caritas Process is not identified as a building block for Caritas Leadership practice in acute care settings?

    a) Caritas Process #3: Transpersonal presence; cultivating own spiritual practices

    b) Caritas Process #5: Authentically listening to another person's story

    c) Caritas Process #6: Creatively problem-solving—"solution-seeking"; creative use of self and all ways of knowing/being/doing/becoming

    d) Caritas Process #10: Open to spiritual, mystery, unknowns—allowing for miracles

9.  Which answer does not pertain to Caritas Leadership in the academy?

   a) Caritas Leadership is grounded on a relational ontology and embraces collaboration.

   b) Caritas Leadership is crucial to advance nursing as both a discipline and a profession.

   c) Caritas leaders have a vision and already know what is best for the people they lead.

   d) Caritas leaders are social activists, inspiring, collaborating, sojourning with others—students, nurse educators, professors, administrators, community, government, and decision-makers.

10. Which answer is the most accurate?

   a) Caritas leaders embrace equity.

   b) Caritas leaders advocate for others to develop their voice.

   c) Caritas leaders create opportunities for others to claim their power.

   d) All the answers above are accurate.

# PROMOTING EXCEPTIONAL PATIENT EXPERIENCE THROUGH COMPASSIONATE CONNECTED CARE®

## REFLECTIVE QUESTIONS

1. What is an important distinction between empathy and compassion?

_____

_____

_____

_____

_____

2.  Why are patient experience surveys important to patient care?

_____

_____

_____

_____

_____

3.  How can practicing the 56-second connection improve patient care?

_____

_____

_____

_____

_____

4.  Why is expert-level AI important to analyze patients' words reflecting their care experiences?

_____

_____

_____

_____

5.  How does AI make it possible to create a narrative evidence basis for human caring?

_____

_____

_____

_____

_____

# NARRATIVE

Community General Hospital is experiencing downward trending over the past two years for both patient experience and caregiver engagement scores. Organizational annual goals have included targets for selected patient experience, key performance indicators such as nurse communication scores and likelihood to recommend the hospital, and intent to leave the organization as a global measure of workforce engagement. Leaders used a number of tactical approaches to improve both engagement and patient experience scores. While efforts have sometimes resulted in temporary improvement, these gains do not last. Staff and leaders are frustrated as they are working hard to provide good patient care and to engage and support staff and caregivers.

# RESPONSE TO NARRATIVE

How might they change their improvement approach to achieve success?

_____

_____

_____

_____

_____

_____

_____

_____

# QUIZ QUESTIONS

1.  Compassion and empathy are interchangeable terms.

    a) True

    b) False

2.  Empathy can be learned.

    a) True

    b) False

3.  The Compassionate Connected Care model for the patient includes which of the following domains?

    a) Caring

    b) Operational

    c) Clinical

    d) All the above

4.  Caregivers may also experience suffering.

    a) True

    b) False

5.  Which of the following outcomes are impacted by using an empathic, patient-centered approach to care?

    a) Patient experience scores

    b) Caregiver engagement scores

    c) Both a & b

    d) Neither a nor b

6.  AI analysis of narrative data should include:

    a) Sentiment analysis

    b) Categorization

    c) Both a & b

    d) Neither a nor b

7.  What did Clavelle et al.'s (2019) study identify as the top theme of extraordinary nursing care in their AI analysis of patients' comments about excellent nurses?

    a) Professionalism

    b) Punctuality

    c) Courtesy & respect

    d) Skill & knowledge

8.  The larger the number of distinct insights that AI can extract per comment, the better it can identify the root causes behind patients' positive or negative experiences.

      a) True

      b) False

9.  Ideally, for expert-level AI, the unit of analysis for sentiment and categorization should be a:

      a) Sentence

      b) Phrase

      c) Section

      d) Paragraph

10. By allowing us to hear what patients say in large volumes, AI makes it possible to create a _____ for the science and practice of human caring.

      a) Pedagogical model

      b) Specific formula

      c) Different language

      d) Narrative evidence basis

# ADDITIONAL RESOURCES: SELECTED VIDEOS AND WEBSITES

- Care Stories: Reducing Patient Suffering (https://www.youtube.com/watch?v=HKx2u3bVbTY)

- The Nursing Advantage: Delivering Compassionate Connected Care (https://www.youtube.com/watch?v=WCx-2qeEHvI&ab_channel=PressGaneyAssociatesLLC)

- Experiences of Care: Reducing Suffering through Compassionate, Connected Care (https://www.youtube.com/watch?v=wmMlb8iIczM&ab_channel=PressGaneyAssociatesLLC)

- 56 Seconds to Create a Connection (https://pressganey.wistia.com/medias/hcxubjvyfz)

- The Schwartz Center (https://www.theschwartzcenter.org/)

- The Power of Empathy: Helen Riess TED Talk (https://www.youtube.com/watch?v=baHrcC8B4WM)

# 12

# APPLYING COMPLEXITY SCIENCE IN PROMOTING COMMUNITY AND POPULATION HEALTH

## REFLECTIVE QUESTIONS

1. From your knowledge and experience, how would you describe healthcare as a complex system and the relationship to complexity theory?

_____

_____

_____

_____

_____

2.   Describe population and community health as a complex adaptive system from a nurse leader's perspective as described in this chapter.

_____

_____

_____

_____

_____

3.   Describe global threats and/or disaster examples that can benefit from complexity leadership as described in this chapter.

_____

_____

_____

_____

_____

4.   Identify at least two actions suggested in the chapter to assist with skill acquisition or increased participation in population health initiatives or health policy development.

a)

_____

_____

b)

_____

_____

5.  What is at least one resource you can utilize from this chapter to assist you with conducting health policy assessments and foster your participation in health policy development?

_____

_____

_____

_____

_____

# NARRATIVE

The Chief Nursing Officer, Senior Charge Nurse, and staff nurses of the obstetric department in a Chinese children's hospital collaborated with a US nurse scientist in a research project in Qingdao, China (Yu et al., 2021). The nursing team identified the breastfeeding rate (17.9%) in their hospital was much lower than the national rate in China (23%), which is a work in progress toward the World Health Organization goal of 50% by 2025 (WHO, 2018). Utilizing project data, the exclusive breastfeeding rate of premature infants was 1.8% and contributed to the separation between mothers and premature infants who were admitted to the Newborn Intensive Care Unit (NICU). From a population health perspective, the team understood, breastfeeding is associated with decreased risk for many early-life diseases and conditions, such as otitis media, respiratory tract infections, asthma, and sudden infant death syndrome. The project team identified gaps between best practice and current practice and the components involved in breastfeeding NICU newborns. From a complex adaptive system perspective and process review, interviews with 17 staff nurses revealed a lack of breastmilk storage equipment in the unit. Interviews with 70 mothers demonstrated they had limited visitation time, which restricted their breastfeeding time in the NICU. These system components, relationships, and interconnections provided a better understanding of the issue's complexity and ultimately encouraged new ways of thinking and practices within this unit. Innovative changes achieved increased education for nurses and mothers on breastfeeding; new processes led to new governance (policies); and improved health outcomes are yielding an improvement in breastfeeding among premature newborns rates from 17.9% to 52.7% (exceeding the WHO goal of 50%) and the exclusive breastfeeding rates from 1.8% to 4.1% over a three-year period. In addition, this case demonstrated international nurses collaborating in critical research, which improved health outcomes.

Yu, G., Liu, F., Zhao, Y., Kong, Y., & Wei, H. (2021). Promoting breastfeeding and lactation among mothers of premature newborns in a hospital in China. *Nursing for Women's Health, 25*(1), 21–29. https://doi.org/10.1016/j.nwh.2020.11.005

# RESPONSE TO THE NARRATIVE

1.  Please explain the nurses' roles in promoting population health in this case.

    _____

    _____

    _____

    _____

    _____

2.  How did systems thinking operationalize changes in this clinical setting?

    _____

    _____

    _____

    _____

    _____

3.  Explain how complex adaptive systems (CAS) thinking determined several needed changes to enhance NICU breastfeeding rates.

    _____

    _____

    _____

    _____

    _____

# QUIZ QUESTIONS

1.  A complex adaptive system has the following characteristics:

    a) Distributed control

    b) Connectivity

    c) Co-evolution

    d) Emergent order

    e) All above

2.  Historically, healthcare organizations operate as a manufactory and machinery, with strict hierarchical power, rules, and assembly lines.

    a) True

    b) False

3.  The traditional rigid and hierarchical organizational structures offer the structure and flexibility needed for production, innovation, and creation.

    a) True

    b) False

4.  Population and community health requires:

    a) A clear-cut strategy to improve effectiveness

    b) A hierarchical structure to allow high productivity

    c) Global connection and collaboration to promote population health

    d) Everyone working independently to ensure efficiency

5.  A great facilitator granting legitimacy in global and population health is:

    a) The friend relationship with influential leaders

    b) A dynamic policy process with minimum specifications

    c) A precise rule-following policy

    d) The continuation of the current protocol

6.  Nurses are a major healthcare workforce and can work most effectively within the profession.

    a) True

    b) False

7.  The dynamic and collaborative process of population management lends itself to complexity science and involves the basic principles, including _____.

      a) Adaptiveness

      b) Emergency

      c) Non-linearity

      d) Connectivity

      e) All the above

8.  In disaster management and building the social infrastructure of adaptive response, intervention strategies at the macro-level can promote population health and community resilience.

      a) True

      b) False

9.  During a global population threat, such as COVID-19, the nursing profession functions at its best if nurses take the following actions except:

      a) Be aware of health policies at the global level

      b) Be aware of government policies

      c) Pay close attention only to the local community

      d) Be involved in policy advocacy

10.  In the US Public Health Service, government actions include:

      a) Public health surveillance of disease

      b) Free health access for the poor and elderly

      c) Evaluation of health promotion programs

      d) Research and education

      e) All the above

# 13

# ASSEMBLING A UNIFYING FORCE: INTERPROFESSIONAL COLLABORATION TO IMPROVE HEALTHCARE

## REFLECTIVE QUESTIONS

1. Eisler and Potter (2014) applied cultural transformation theory to healthcare systems and described how those systems fall along a continuum from domination- to partnership-based systems. List characteristics specific to a domination-based system.

_____

_____

_____

_____

_____

2. List characteristics specific to a partnership-based system.

_____

_____

_____

_____

_____

3. Consider how a domination system impacts the patient experience within healthcare environments. Read the following example and then answer the question.

Emely was 5. She and her mother, Lydia, were scared. Emely was admitted to the hospital for chronic leg pain, and they both had a lot of questions. As a non-native English speaker, Lydia did the best she could to understand the nurses and physicians when they told her that Emely would have labs done, various tests, and possible treatments. The healthcare team made little attempt to ensure that Lydia understood what they were saying, and rarely included her in any decisions. She continued to ask questions and seek partnership from the team during the journey but didn't even know what questions to ask. Behind closed doors, the physicians discussed the cancer diagnosis and asked that the nurses not discuss it with the family. They withheld the information for four days. On a Friday afternoon, the healthcare team took 10 minutes to tell Lydia that Emely was diagnosed with cancer. Lydia was alone in the room with Emely; no support persons were present. She was left with more questions than she initially had and felt too rushed to ask anything. Whom could she turn to about her fears when so far no one had made the effort to listen, to work in partnership, to truly care for them? Lydia and Emely felt alone.

List some ways in which the healthcare team exhibited domination characteristics during the care of Lydia and Emely.

_____

_____

_____

_____

_____

4.   Read the following example from a partnership-based perspective and then answer the following questions.

Emely was 5. She and her mother, Lydia, were scared. Emely was admitted to the hospital for chronic leg pain, and they both had a lot of questions. The healthcare team immediately recognized the need for an interpreter and arranged one to be present as they discussed with Lydia all the labs that could be done, various tests, and possible treatments. They asked her if she needed other resources or support during this time. Lydia and Emely discussed their fears with the healthcare team. Each day the healthcare team would discuss any new information or change in plans, including them in all the decisions. Once they identified that it was in fact cancer, the healthcare team held a meeting to discuss the information with Lydia as her family surrounded her. They supported Lydia as she asked her questions and provided her with resources in case more questions came up afterwards. Lydia and Emely knew they could turn to their healthcare team at any time with their fears and questions as the team had made every effort to listen, to work in partnership, and to truly care for them. Lydia and Emely felt safe.

List some ways in which the healthcare team exhibited partnership-based characteristics during the care of Lydia and Emely.

_____

_____

_____

_____

_____

5.   How can partnership-based systems be used to transform healthcare at the bedside, in communities, across nations, and even the health of the planet?

_____

_____

_____

_____

_____

# NARRATIVE

You are the Director of Public Health for a county in Northern California. Climate change is causing frequent and severe heat waves with high temperatures throughout the day and very little relief in the evenings. You are aware of numerous families living in older apartment buildings without air-conditioning, and their indoor temperatures are continuing to rise. In addition, heavy winter snows led to massive growth of brush which has now dried and is fueling predictions that this will be a very severe fire year.

You are aware that your county has an aging population with many chronic health issues. In addition to wildfires and severe heat, fires bring days with unhealthy air quality, which can be especially dangerous for people with asthma and other chronic lung diseases.

Climate change impacts the health of populations, but it also impacts the health of individuals. Recently one of the county's visiting nurses raised a concern about an insulin-dependent diabetic. The packaging for the insulin says "keep it at room temperature of 20–25°C (68–77°F) after opening. DO NOT store in the refrigerator." Without air-conditioning, indoor temperatures are no longer less than 77 degrees. Is this patient safe?

# RESPONSE TO THE NARRATIVE

1.  Make a list of the actual and potential health issues in this scenario. Define "health" broadly using a planetary health lens.

    _____

    _____

    _____

    _____

    _____

2.  Choose one health problem and address the following questions.

    a) When forming an interprofessional team to address this problem, which health professions need to be included?

    _____

    _____

    _____

    _____

    _____

b) When forming a transdisciplinary team to address this problem, which disciplines and stakeholders need to be included?

_____

_____

_____

_____

_____

c) You know that it is essential for all ideas and all voices to be heard if the teams are to create the transformative changes that are necessary. List two group norms that you can suggest, encouraging teams to work in partnership rather than hierarchies of domination.

_____

_____

_____

_____

_____

# QUIZ QUESTIONS

1. In 1972, the Institute of Medicine (IOM) issued the first report proposing that high-quality care for patients living with chronic illness requires a team approach.

   a) True

   b) False

2. Leaders in partnership-based systems are appointed based on ranking rather than expertise.

   a) True

   b) False

3. Key factors required for interprofessional practice include the following: (mark all that apply)

   a) Understanding that each discipline makes a unique contribution to the team.

   b) Understanding the roles and responsibilities of each profession.

   c) Team members need to share the same physical space for interprofessional collaboration.

   d) The nurse-physician dyad is the primary leadership nucleus of interprofessional care.

4. Planetary health is described by the following statements: (mark all that apply)

    a) The nursing profession recognizes that the environment is part of the healing paradigm.

    b) Transdisciplinary research is needed to create effective solutions.

    c) The primary purpose of planetary health is to address climate change.

    d) The health of humans and the health of the planet are deeply interconnected.

5. Global nursing leaders have collaborated in partnership to create Nurses Drawdown (NDD). Which of the following statements are correct? (mark all that apply)

    a) NDD solutions focus on improving the health of the planet, not human health.

    b) NDD teaches nurses about evidence-based solutions to drawdown greenhouse gases.

    c) Nurses are encouraged to bring NDD solutions to patients, families, and communities.

6. Cuban healthcare relies on a government-run public health system that, despite limited resources, has similar or better outcomes than other industrialized countries.

    a) True

    b) False

7. The following statements describe the Cuban healthcare system: (select all that apply)

    a) Consultorios offer primary care delivered by collaborative teams in neighborhood settings. These teams provide care for up to 700–1,500 residents in their area.

    b) The Cuban healthcare model can easily be transferred to any country and be effective.

    c) There is a focus on the health of the community through disease prevention and wellness education.

    d) Polyclinicas form the second tier of the Cuban healthcare system and provide more advanced specialty care.

    e) Cuba's public health success is based on ample healthcare and economic resources.

8. An interprofessional education offering is defined as an activity where a minimum of four or more healthcare professionals learn with, from, and about each other with a focus on improving collaboration and quality of care.

    a) True

    b) False

9. Health professionals contribute informally to collaboration with each other by three essential actions: bridging professional and social gaps between each other, negotiating overlapping roles and tasks, and creating spaces to be able to work effectively in teams.

    a) True

    b) False

10.  The following are examples of interprofessional collaborative practice: (mark all that apply)

   a) Leadership is based on rank and use of top-down communication flow.

   b) Interprofessional collaborative teams that use telehealth for care conferences.

   c) Team-based community clinic care of a patient with multiple psychosocial needs.

   d) Complex care for acutely ill patients in the hospital setting.

   e) The role of nurses is to support physician-led teams.

# LEADERSHIP IN DISASTER PREPAREDNESS AND RESPONSE

## REFLECTIVE QUESTIONS

1.  Why do disaster nurses need to minimize personal and moral conflicts that may occur in disaster response and recovery?

   _____

   _____

   _____

   _____

   _____

2.  During disaster response and recovery, nurses may be asked by the Incident Commander (IC) to be a part of a non-healthcare-related disaster team or asked to complete tasks that are not nursing-related, such as debris removal or food distribution. How should nurse leaders respond to these requests and the potential implications of both accepting and declining the assignment?

_____

_____

_____

_____

_____

3.  Discuss vulnerable populations and special considerations nurse leaders must include in disaster preparation, mitigation, response, and recovery.

_____

_____

_____

_____

_____

4.  Community members have many spiritual, cultural, and ethnic differences. Considering your community population and their ethnic and cultural differences, how would you plan for these differences in the disaster preparation process?

_____

_____

_____

_____

_____

5.   What are your community's strengths and resources for disaster preparation? What are key challenges and mitigation measures to address those challenges?

_____

_____

_____

_____

_____

# ACTIVITY

In a group, review the scenario below and then identify the resources needed to respond to the disaster effectively. Each student will assume a different incident command leadership role based on the community needs they identify and present their request for resources based on what they believe is necessary to safely assist their community.

**Scenario:** Emerald Place is a small, quaint coastal community with a population of 3,000 people that enjoys tourists from all over the world in the summer months. During the summer months, the population increases to over 10,000, including visitors. The town has a popular waterfront area, which sits at sea level, with many locally-owned retail shops that sell local crafts, clothing, coffee, and baked goods, along with several excellent seafood restaurants. Tourists enjoy staying at the many bed and breakfasts and historic homes rented through online rental websites. The town has a mayor, five town commissioners, a town manager, and support staff. They have combined police, fire, and rescue department with eight police officers, 10 paid firefighters with two fire trucks, and two rescue squads manned with emergency medical technicians. The electricity is operated by a large corporation located four hours away. The town has a district public water plant that supplies 90% of the population. The remaining 10% have personal wells. There is one main internet provider that services the area. There are three schools: one elementary, one middle, and one high school. The nearest hospital is 30 miles away in a larger city. There are two primary healthcare offices, two pharmacies, and one dentist in the town. There are two grocery stores, one locally owned hardware store, and a lumber store. Most local residents travel to other towns to work, with a 30-mile commute at a minimum. The local population is predominately English-speaking, with 50% of the residents under the age of 65.

On August 20th, a hurricane has formed in the Atlantic Ocean. As the storm nears, it strengthens. The projected path is within 50 miles of Emerald Place, with anticipated landfall in 96 hours. Based on the information provided, you are responsible for forming a disaster response team and making initial preparations.

Here are some questions to consider. Use the space below to jot down possible responses to share with your group.

1.  What are the hazards, threats, and risks?

    _____

    _____

    _____

    _____

    _____

2.  Who would you need on your team?

    _____

    _____

    _____

    _____

    _____

3.  What resources do you need?

    _____

    _____

    _____

    _____

    _____

4.    What are the concerns you identify that would need to be addressed?

_____

_____

_____

_____

_____

5.    What are the priorities for the disaster management team?

_____

_____

_____

_____

_____

# RESPONSE TO THE ACTIVITY

Use the space below to reflect upon the activity.

_____

_____

_____

_____

_____

_____

_____

# QUIZ QUESTIONS

1.  When determining if an event qualifies as a disaster, the key determinant is the size of the event.

    a) True

    b) False

2.  Disaster management is proactive in planning and reactive, when necessary, as all potential threats and hazards cannot be reasonably anticipated.

    a) True

    b) False

3.  All community members must be accepted into disaster emergency shelters regardless of their medical conditions.

    a) True

    b) False

4.  Nurses are licensed to practice in any state where a formal disaster declaration has been made.

    a) True

    b) False

5.  Church facilities or community buildings may be used to meet temporary housing needs for medically fragile residents.

    a) True

    b) False

6.  The primary goals of disaster management include which of the following:

    a) Reduce loss of life

    b) Minimize property damage

    c) Minimize environmental damage

    d) All the above

7.  A well-developed disaster plan will include the key missions listed below except which of the following?

    a) Prevention

    b) Protection

    c) Mitigation

    d) Communication

    e) Recovery

8.  Extreme cold temperatures have been predicted in a community, and authorization by the county health director has been given to open a warming shelter from sundown to sunrise for the following three nights. Which level of nursing response is required to assist?

   a) Level I—Basic RN education

   b) Level II—Some specialized education in disaster management

   c) Level III—Advanced education in disaster management

   d) None of the above—nurses do not need to be involved

9.  Personal causes of psychological distress that may manifest during a disaster include:

   a) Lack of electricity impacting communication efforts

   b) Lack of cash on hand for purchases of food, supplies, and medications

   c) Misinformation from social media on available resources

   d) All the above

10. This part of disaster planning involves health surveillance aimed at tracking communicable diseases, health risks, and subsequent chronic diseases. Select the best answer.

   a) Continuity of Operations Plan

   b) Geographic Information System

   c) Disaster Epidemiology

   d) National Incident Management System

# 15

# NURSING LEADERSHIP IN THE GLOBAL HEALTH CONTEXT

## REFLECTIVE QUESTIONS

1. Please discuss why it is important for nurse leaders to understand the macro-level implications of policies.

_____

_____

_____

_____

_____

_____

_____

2.  How does Rao and Kelleher's (2005) gender-specific framework offer insight into empowering women and transforming change across societies?

_____

_____

_____

_____

_____

3.  What are three characteristics that would be needed of a globally minded nursing and midwifery leader?

    a)

_____

_____

_____

    b)

_____

_____

_____

    c)

_____

_____

_____

4.   Explain the importance or lack thereof of the nursing profession within global health governance.

_____

_____

_____

_____

_____

_____

_____

5.   What are three ways nurses can increase their skill set in becoming more globally minded and politically conscious?

a)

_____

_____

_____

b)

_____

_____

_____

c)

_____

_____

_____

# ACTIVITY

**Scenario:** Janet is a 28-year-old staff nurse who has been a nurse for six years. She has primarily worked in an acute care setting with older geriatric patients dealing with chronic diseases for most of her career. Recently she has become more interested in working internationally and relocating abroad to use her skill set in a different country. She has seen job postings for leadership and managerial positions with global health organizations. Still, she is not sure how to gain experience to be a viable candidate for those jobs. She does not have any experience working in global health but recently saw an advertisement for an international conference in her city and decided it might be a great way to network and meet people connected to and working in global health. This is Janet's first conference that is not specifically focused on her clinical expertise and not exclusively for nurses.

At the conference's networking social, she feels isolated, anxious, and inadequate since she does not have any global health experience and she does not know anyone at this event. But she also realizes this is an excellent opportunity, as numerous international organizations with employment opportunities and major players in global health are in attendance.

Activity: Within your group, each of you should assume the role of a first-time attendee at an international global health conference.

# RESPONSE TO THE ACTIVITY

1.  How would you advise Janet to approach networking at this social?

_____

_____

_____

_____

_____

_____

_____

_____

_____

_____

2.  How can Janet leverage and highlight her clinical expertise among a group of non-nurse clinicians?

_____

_____

_____

_____

_____

3.  How can Janet prepare for future conferences and networking opportunities to maximize her experience?

_____

_____

_____

_____

_____

_____

4.  Reflect on how isolated Janet feels about not having many nursing colleagues around and being outside of her "comfort zone." What are ways to create a more inclusive environment within your own workplace, network, and organization?

_____

_____

_____

_____

_____

_____

_____

_____

_____

# QUIZ QUESTIONS

1.  Networking is an important tool to expand opportunities for nurses.

    a) True

    b) False

2.  Which of the following will allow you to be better prepared for conferences and networking events?

    a) Bring business cards

    b) Utilize social media to post about the conference

    c) Have a goal when attending the conference

    d) All the above

3.  Which of the following statements would not be a conversation starter at a conference or networking event?

    a) Where are you from?

    b) Have you attended the conference before?

    c) Can you offer me a job?

    d) What has been your favorite session thus far?

4.  Janet's bedside clinical experience would not be an asset when highlighting her clinical expertise.

    a) True

    b) False

5.  Email is an appropriate avenue to following up with contacts met at a conference.

    a) True

    b) False

6.  Self-reflection is an important aspect to consider before making your environments (work, professional, and personal) more inclusive.

    a) True

    b) False

7.  Which of the following could be a possible location to find a list of conference attendees to plan meetings and networking opportunities?

    a) Conference abstract

    b) Social media

    c) None of the above

    d) Both a and b

8.  Which of the following are ways to create a more inclusive environment within your network?

    a) Improve your listening skills

    b) Join social clubs outside your professional interests

    c) Utilize your existing network to make introductions

    d) Both a and c

9.  Which of the following statements exemplify Janet leveraging her clinical expertise at the global health conference?

    a) "I do not have any global health experience."

    b) "Although I am new to global health, I have had six years of experience caring for patients, working within a healthcare system, and I have a good understanding of the challenges of care delivery in an urban setting."

    c) "I came to this conference to learn about global health."

    d) "What qualifications are you looking for to hire people at your organization?"

10. Having a diverse network of personal contacts can be one effective strategy to increasing your professional connections.

    a) True

    b) False

# HEALTHCARE LEADERSHIP IN PROMOTING THE USE OF EVIDENCE

## REFLECTIVE QUESTIONS

1. What happens when leaders and clinicians conduct their roles without using the best evidence to inform their thinking and actions?

   _____

   _____

   _____

   _____

   _____

2. Given what you learned from this chapter, how can healthcare systems better support their leaders and clinicians in the application of best evidence for their decisions and practice?

   _____

   _____

   _____

   _____

3.  What would you identify as the first three actions that need to be taken by nurse managers so that they can effectively influence clinicians to use evidence-based practice in the clinical setting?

    a)

    _____

    _____

    _____

    b)

    _____

    _____

    _____

    c)

    _____

    _____

    _____

4.  What gets in the way of your own use of best evidence in your daily practice, and what steps can you take to remove these barriers?

    _____

    _____

    _____

    _____

    _____

5.  What would quality, safe care look like if best evidence and processes were used consistently by leaders and staff?

_____

_____

_____

_____

_____

# NARRATIVE

In 2014, the department of nursing at Memorial Sloan Kettering (MSK), an ANCC Magnet designated and NCI designated comprehensive cancer center, underwent organizational changes at the executive nursing level. The Senior Vice President and Chief Nursing Officer (SVP CNO) reorganized the divisions of nursing practice, quality, and education under the newly created office of the Deputy Chief Nursing Officer (DCNO). One of the deliverables the DCNO was given was to create, launch, and sustain an evidence-based practice (EBP) infrastructure across the nursing enterprise. As an internationally recognized oncology nursing service, these leaders believed that applying evidence to nursing care delivery would ensure MSK's leadership position in oncology nursing practice. Using a high-reliability framework, the DCNO set out to strengthen the department's approach to EBP. Leadership commitment was foundational to the full actualization of the vision and to ensure sustained EBP competency for every nurse across the care continuum. A partnership with the Helene Fuld Health Trust National Institute for Evidence-based Practice (EBP) was put in motion to leverage an innovative, deliberate, and customized college-level EBP immersion for the nursing enterprise at MSK. At the outset, a pivotal decision was made by the DCNO: all nursing leadership, inclusive of CNO, DCNO, Nursing Directors, Nurse Leaders, CNSs, Nursing Professional Development Specialists, and Quality Management Nurses, would be required to attend the first EBP immersion together as a cohort. This ensured all the nursing leadership was learning the method simultaneously, which would mitigate any skepticism and roadblocks to successful EBP adoption. Without leadership engagement and buy-in, the DCNO believed immersion across the enterprise would be futile. Because all nursing leadership was required to participate in the immersion, a safety net was created in the event one level of leadership failed to buy into the enculturation. This unique approach fostered collegial relationships, broke down existing silos, strengthened the department, and built a unique EBP capacity with the goal of preparing all MSK nurses in an established EBP methodology, building EBP competence, and making evidence-based decision-making the standard practice across the nursing enterprise.

Additional deliberate strategies were required to ensure the adoption of EBP at MSK. Recognizing Clinical Nurse Specialists as EBP experts and early adopters, structural changes were necessary to actualize the full vision. In January 2017, the CNS reporting structure was centralized to strengthen, support, and sustain a spirit and culture of inquiry across the care continuum. The vision for EBP enculturation included a call to validate existing policies, procedures, and standards of care and challenge the "Memorial Way" to ensure the existing nursing practice was up to date and in alignment with the evidence and best practice. Collaboration with the well-established and expert team from the Fuld Institute was pivotal to bringing EBP structures and processes to every chairside, bedside, and tableside across the care continuum.

The EBP immersions consisted of a standard curriculum provided by the EBP Institute's faculty and facilitation of implementation by Fuld expert mentors. Multiple cohorts attended the immersion program, with each subsequent cohort strategically assembled to move EBP expertise beyond the leadership cadre by thoughtfully including academic and alliance partners, staff nurses, and interdisciplinary colleagues. All participants were assigned to one of three unique learning tracks in the program: mentor, leader, or academic. Post immersion, each cohort met with a Fuld EBP expert for follow-up and boosters every three months for 15 months. These sessions were focused on feedback, direction, and support. During this same time, the adoption of EBP terminology and methods were introduced across the department and incorporated into shared governance bylaws and promotional and staff development processes. MSK Librarians developed resources for writing PICO questions and offered courses on evidence searching and reference management. Cohort groups presented their 15-month-long work at a peer symposium/celebration. EBP initiative presentations included clinical inquiry, PICO questions, critical appraisal of the body of evidence conducted, synthesis tables, and evidence-based recommendations for practice or administrative changes to be implemented. Many recommendations have been fully implemented and sustained, and whenever appropriate, measurements of clinical outcomes, value, and returns on investments have been reported.

The strategy of leadership engagement first promoted the enculturation of EBP institution-wide and led to measurable outcomes on challenging clinical/institutional initiatives such as falls, handoff, mindfulness, inpatient discharge, palliative care, opioid addiction in the oncology patient, extravasations, etc. To date, more than 60 EBP initiatives have emerged. A measured increase in knowledge of EBP was appreciated because of the intensive immersion. Surveys of knowledge and skill acquisition and attitude about EBP demonstrated a significant change from baseline. A second, unpredicted outcome was that the immersion sparked interest from participants in returning to advanced degree programs.

MSK nursing leadership now utilizes a systematic process for translating evidence into practice. Capitalizing on this new skill set has led to confirmation of existing best practice/policy as well as to bringing novel EBP interventions forward to address universal, ongoing, and problematic clinical issues. The initial leadership immersion became the foundation for embedding EBP into the culture of MSK. Leadership has demonstrated a sustained commitment to the EBP process as mentors, facilitators, and advocates, ultimately impacting patient care in such a positive and meaningful way.

# RESPONSE TO THE NARRATIVE

What do you think are the most important leadership actions in this exemplar?

_____

_____

_____

_____

_____

_____

_____

_____

_____

_____

# REFLECTIVE QUESTIONS

1. Describe how a partnership with the Helene Fuld Health Trust National Institute for Evidence-based Practice (EBP) impacted the success of the MSK EBP journey.

_____

_____

_____

_____

_____

_____

_____

2.  Why was engaging all MSK's nursing leaders as the first EBP cohort so critical to MSK's success?

_____

_____

_____

_____

_____

_____

_____

3.  What are some key leadership strategies that have sustained EBP at MSK?

_____

_____

_____

_____

_____

_____

_____

4.  List three important outcomes that can be actualized when nurse leaders take a systematic approach to developing an evidence-based approach to care.

a)

_____

_____

_____

b)

_____

_____

_____

c)

_____

_____

_____

# QUIZ QUESTIONS

1.  Name the four domains of the use of evidence.

    a)

    _____

    b)

    _____

    c)

    _____

    d)

    _____

2.  What is the difference between research and evidence-based practice (EBP)?

    _____

    _____

    _____

    _____

    _____

3.  Despite a multitude of studies demonstrating that its use leads to quality, safe patient care, which of the four domains is still not hardwired and used throughout operations in healthcare and why?

    _____

    _____

    _____

    _____

    _____

4.  Who is critical for the integration and sustainability of EBP?

    _____

    _____

    _____

    _____

    _____

5.  How can clinicians be supported to use/apply evidence in their daily practice?

    _____

    _____

    _____

    _____

    _____

6. For an organization to be successful in integrating the continuum of best practices and processes to deliver outcomes, what two things must be in place?

_____

_____

_____

_____

_____

7. What are the three broad categories that characterize the role of the nurse leader to promote the use of EBP by clinicians in their daily practice?

   a) Leading the way for EBP, building an infrastructure for EBP, managing the process for EBP

   b) Building an infrastructure for EBP, determining readiness for EBP, promoting EBP

   c) Leading EBP, building infrastructure for EBP, promoting EBP

8. Name one organizational model that focuses on the systemwide process for implementation for EBP discussed in this chapter.

_____

_____

9. Name one practice change model used to implement EBP discussed in this chapter.

_____

_____

10. Which is correct regarding the implications for the consistent use of evidence in making clinician decisions/actions?

   a) Only when the use of evidence is the standard of practice will the Quadruple Aim in health be achieved.

   b) Nurse leaders who achieve competency in EBP will make effective decisions that can result in achieving targeted outcomes.

   c) Leaders who use EBP create future leaders who will use EBP.

   d) All the above

# ADDITIONAL RESOURCES: SELECTED WEBSITES AND VIDEOS

Conversations on Wisdom: Uncut Interview with Robert Sternberg (https://www.youtube.com/watch?v=8ZlStKt8wN8&ab_channel=UniversityofChicagoCenterforPractialWisdom)

Harthill Consulting (https://www.harthill.co.uk/)

University of Chicago Center for Practical Wisdom (https://wisdomcenter.uchicago.edu/about)

Project Wisdom (https://www.projectwisdom.com/ERS/Introduction.asp)

Wisdom Research YouTube Channel (https://www.youtube.com/channel/UCaT5a5nYYbm4z5gTP-KF6SXg)

The Co-Intelligence Institute (https://www.co-intelligence.org/)

The VIA Institute on Character (https://www.viacharacter.org/)

Interview with Angela Barron McBride, Katherine Densford International Center for Nursing Leadership Summit of Sages Archives (https://www.youtube.com/watch?v=zmci5YBXSGU&list=PLQ49nIC7ESoD_KSaaNaG33WqrxCN8a55A&index=5)

Lessons in Leadership Interview with Angela Barron McBride (https://sigma.nursingrepository.org/handle/10755/582319 or https://www.youtube.com/watch?v=sb-smgE71l0)

# WISDOM LEADERSHIP: A DEVELOPMENTAL JOURNEY

## REFLECTIVE QUESTIONS

1. What did you appreciate about the discussion of wisdom leadership presented in this chapter?

_____

_____

_____

_____

_____

2. How did ideas and material presented influence your thinking and feeling?

_____

_____

_____

_____

3.    What if any commitments to action will you make because of reading this chapter?

_____

_____

_____

_____

_____

4.    How might you apply the Balance Theory of Wisdom to a leadership issue you are currently trying to influence and manage?

_____

_____

_____

_____

_____

5.    What aspects of the Balance Theory of Wisdom definition are you dealing with successfully?
What needs more attention?

_____

_____

_____

_____

_____

6. As you reflect on the adult cognitive developmental stages presented in this work, what is your personal assessment of your current stage of development?

_____

_____

_____

_____

_____

7. In your own words, how do you explain the differences between horizontal and vertical leadership development?

_____

_____

_____

_____

_____

8. Read and reflect on Nic Petrie's 2015 article, "The How to of Vertical Leadership Development" (https://www.stageshift.coach/resource_redirect/downloads/sites/1193/themes/1903840/downloads/XwpFxnoQUmeOfyLVdXif_Nick_Petrie_CCL_2015_The_How_of_Vertical_Development_Part_II.pdf)

Which of the 15 approaches Petrie suggests are of interest to you and relevant to your leadership development plans?

_____

_____

_____

_____

_____

9.  What are strategies one can use to teach wisdom or develop wisdom capacities with students, peers, and/or colleagues?

    _____

    _____

    _____

    _____

    _____

# QUIZ QUESTIONS

1.  Wisdom capacities include the ability to reflect, forgive, and be humble, trustworthy, compassionate, relationship-oriented, and positive.

    a) True

    b) False

2.  Wisdom capacities include the ability to problem solve and get to a right answer given a challenge or issue to solve.

    a) True

    b) False

3.  Wise leaders ask different questions, seek multiple perspectives, and see and think in systems.

    a) True

    b) False

4.  The action logic of impulsivity can be classified at what stage of adult cognitive development?

    a) Pre-conventional

    b) Conventional

    c) Post-conventional

5.  The action logic of strategist can be classified at what stage of adult cognitive development?

    a) Pre-conventional

    b) Conventional

    c) Post-conventional

6. A wise person has learned to balance three aspects of behavior: cognition, affect, and volition.

   a) True

   b) False

7. Researchers Joiner and Josephs (2006) argue wise and successful leaders master four types of agility related to:

   a) Vision, mission, goals, and strategic plans

   b) Self, context, stakeholders, and creativity

   c) Creating, competing, controlling, and collaborating

   d) Budgets, financial planning, investments, and resource management

8. Horizontal leadership development helps people acquire more intricate and advanced ways of thinking and perspective taking.

   a) True

   b) False

9. According to Angela Barron McBride there are five stages to a career. The stages are:

   a) Initiating, Development, Collaboration, Cooperation, Independence

   b) Novice, Advanced Beginner, Competent, Proficient, Expert

   c) Preparation, Independent Contributions, Development of Home Setting, Development of the Field, the Gadfly Wise Person Period

   d) Noticing, Reflecting, Interpreting, Responding, Evaluating

10. The Teaching Wisdom Project suggests which of the following procedures to support the teaching of wisdom:

   a) Encourage students to read classic works and reflect on the wisdom of the sages.

   b) Engage students in discussion about what they have read and how lessons learned can be applied in their own lives.

   c) Challenge students to think about their own values and how their values influence their thinking and reasoning.

   d) Encourage students to consider the role of critical, creative, and practical thinking when confronted with challenges and dilemmas.

   e) Encourage students to weigh the good and bad outcomes of a course of action with a greater good in mind.

   f) Teachers should role model wise thinking for students as they propose problems, raise questions, and tackle complex dilemmas and situations.

   g) All the above

# 18

# DIVERSITY, EQUITY, AND INCLUSION IN EDUCATION AND HEALTH SYSTEMS

## REFLECTIVE QUESTIONS

1.  Name one way in which racism, discrimination, and inequity reflect in nursing.

    _____

    _____

    _____

    _____

    _____

2.  How can we create safe academic environments to recruit and retain American Indian and other students of color into graduate nursing programs to diversify nursing leadership roles?

_____

_____

_____

_____

_____

3.  How can we remove barriers to promotion and tenure for American Indian and other scholars of color within academic institutions?

_____

_____

_____

_____

_____

4.  How do you foster an inclusive environment for patients and nurses of color in your unit, and what is the role of nurse leaders in promoting inclusive environments?

_____

_____

_____

_____

_____

5.  What is the role of administrative leaders in nursing higher education to engage in racial justice and equity work?

_____

_____

_____

_____

_____

# NARRATIVE

Rachel is a registered nurse on a medical-surgical unit who identifies as African American/Black. At the beginning of her shift Rachel is assigned to a 55-year-old White male patient. During her routine assessments, the patient asked if Rachel could call the nurse to the room. Rachel explained that she is a registered nurse, and she has the necessary training to manage the patient's condition. The patient became upset and asked Rachel to call her supervisor.

You are a nurse manager on a medical-surgical unit. When you enter the room, the patient says: "I do not want a Black nurse. I would prefer to have a White nurse. I am not sure if she knows what she is doing." Rachel also verbalizes to you that she feels discriminated against based on her race despite her competence to carry out the assigned tasks.

# RESPONSE TO THE NARRATIVE

How do you respond to this encounter?

In the space below, answer the following questions.

1.  Describe ways you can assess this situation as part of the de-escalation process.

_____

_____

_____

_____

_____

_____

_____

2.   What are the ethical implications that should be considered in this scenario?

_____

_____

_____

_____

_____

_____

_____

3.   Discuss the process for documenting the patient's refusal of treatment.

_____

_____

_____

_____

_____

_____

_____

4.   What are some effective ways an institution can promote inclusion and recognition for nurses of color on your unit?

_____

_____

_____

_____

_____

_____

5.  List some of the implications that this encounter would have on Rachel and other nurses of color.

_____

_____

_____

_____

_____

_____

_____

# QUIZ QUESTIONS

1.  What are the sources of discrimination for BIPOC nurses on inpatient units?

    a) Patients

    b) Staff

    c) Nurse leaders

    d) All the above

2.  Select the concepts that are important for leaders of nursing schools to understand (choose all that apply).

    a) Intersectionality

    b) Decolonizing perspectives

    c) Anti-racist pedagogy

    d) White privilege and diversity

    e) All the above

3.  Administrators and faculty in schools of nursing currently must demonstrate a baseline level of competency to engage in conversations about diversity.

    a) True

    b) False

4.  Is it OK to assume that an American Indian graduate student in your class can speak on behalf of all American Indians about a particular topic that is being discussed in class?

    a) True

    b) False

5.  Select the concept(s) that are important for leaders of nursing schools to avoid when trying to create a safe environment for BIPOC faculty (choose all that apply).

   a) Resisting colorblindness

   b) Tokenizing BIPOC faculty

   c) Incorporating land acknowledgments into campus policies and procedures

   d) Indigenizing curriculum

6.  Discrimination toward BIPOC patients can result in long-term health consequences.

   a) True

   b) False

7.  What is the best response to a patient who requests to switch their provider from a BIPOC nurse to a White nurse?

   a) Respect patient's rights and switch provider

   b) Decline patient's request and offer transfer if necessary

   c) Have a White and BIPOC nurse share responsibility for the client

   d) All the above

8.  Reflexivity on the part of faculty is valuable to enhancing faculty understanding of their social location in relation to their students and determining how best to create a more nurturing environment that facilitates student success.

   a) True

   b) False

9.  Academic climate is one of the most important factors for the academic success of BIPOC students.

   a) True

   b) False

10.  Intervention(s) that support the success of BIPOC students in nursing academia include:

   a) Listening sessions

   b) Creating safe spaces

   c) Fostering trusting relationships between BIPOC students and faculty

   d) All the above

# 19

# TRANSFORMING HEALTH POLICY

## REFLECTIVE QUESTIONS

1.  Briefly describe the five-phase model of policymaking.

_____

_____

_____

_____

_____

_____

_____

2.  How can nurses play a role in each of the five phases of policymaking?

_____

_____

_____

_____

_____

_____

_____

3.  Describe policy-related activities that nurses can engage in at the individual level.

_____

_____

_____

_____

_____

_____

_____

4.  How do nursing professional organizations participate in the policymaking process?

_____

_____

_____

_____

_____

_____

5.  Name and reflect on sources of power that you possess that you may not have been aware of previously.

_____

_____

_____

_____

_____

_____

_____

# NARRATIVE

Nurse and patient advocacy groups in North Carolina (NC) have been calling for the removal of physician supervisory requirements for NC's advanced practice registered nurses (APRNs). NC law currently requires APRNs to have a collaborative practice agreement with a supervising physician. These physicians do not actually "supervise" or even work in the same location as the APRN, and, in many cases, APRNs must pay physicians to serve as their supervisors. NC is one of only a handful of states that continues to require collaborative practice agreements. APRN education and certification have been standardized nationally since the early 1990s, and research indicates APRNs provide safe, effective care. Research also indicates collaborative practice/supervisory requirements increase the cost of care, decrease access to care, and provide no value to patient care. Yet NC, a rural state where millions of citizens experience significant disparities in healthcare access, continues to restrict the APRN practice.

The NC SAVE Act (NC Senate Bill 249/House Bill 277) would remove physician oversight requirements for NC's APRNs. NC State Representative Gale Adcock, who is a nurse practitioner, introduced the SAVE Act to NC's legislature in the 2021 session. The bill has bipartisan support and is also sponsored by the other three registered nurses who serve in NC's legislature, among other legislative members. Groups supporting the legislation include the North Carolina Nurses Association and its PAC, the AARP North Carolina, Americans for Prosperity North Carolina, the March of Dimes, the National Academy of Medicine, and the Rural Center. Business groups including the Convenient Care Association and Amazon also endorse the bill, citing its potential for improving access to healthcare. Only physician groups oppose the legislation, citing unsubstantiated patient safety concerns.

The NC legislature has considered bills related to APRN supervision several times over the past few years. In past sessions, bills that would have removed APRN practice restrictions died during the legislative session. Nurse and patient advocacy groups hope the bill will be passed this session. The SAVE Act has the bipartisan support of a record number of NC Representatives and Senators. The COVID-19 crisis highlighted the fragility of the state's healthcare system and the importance of increasing healthcare access, particularly in NC's rural regions. Moreover, as part of efforts to increase healthcare access during the COVID-19 crisis, the NC legislature temporarily lifted several restrictions on APRN practice that would be made permanent if the SAVE Act is passed. Lifting these APRN practice restrictions may have illustrated to lawmakers that the restrictions served no purpose but to restrict healthcare access.

## RESPONSE TO THE NARRATIVE

In the space below, answer the following questions.

1.  How do you think nurses, both individually and collectively, helped get the issue of physician oversight of APRNs on the policy agenda? How might their framing of the issue have garnered widespread support?

\
\
\
\
\
\
\

2.  Who are the stakeholders in this legislation, and what do you imagine their concerns are?

\
\
\
\
\
\
\

3.  What can nurses do, both individually and collectively, to encourage members of the NC legislature to vote in favor of the bill?

_____

_____

_____

_____

_____

_____

4.  What role do PACs play? What role do lobbyists play? How could theories about agenda setting help us understand what forces might contribute to the bill's success this session?

_____

_____

_____

_____

_____

_____

# QUIZ QUESTIONS

1.  All the following are stages of the policy process except:

> a) Agenda setting
>
> b) Policy formulation
>
> c) Decision-making
>
> d) Policy implementation
>
> e) The PDSA cycle

2.  Which of the following are in Kingdon's Multiple Streams Theory related to agenda-setting?

    a) Problems or issues

    b) Solutions or policies

    c) Political conditions

    d) All the above

    e) None of the above

3.  A country's political system determines nurses' access to the policymaking process.

    a) True

    b) False

4.  The American Nurses Association comments on draft rules and regulations.

    a) True

    b) False

5.  The terms used when one individual/group has special information that another person/group wants is:

    a) Collective power

    b) Bargaining power

    c) Information power

    d) Coercive power

    e) Positional power

6.  The concept of healthcare as a human right can be used to challenge policies that compromise a human's right to healthcare.

    a) True

    b) False

7.  International non-governmental organizations (INGOs) can engage in political advocacy and national policy processes on behalf of donors.

    a) True

    b) False

8.  Advocating for equity and social justice in resource allocation, access to healthcare, and other social and economic services falls outside the scope of nursing.

    a) True

    b) False

9.  All the following are federal legislative priorities of the American Nurses Association except:

    a) Safe staffing

    b) COVID-19

    c) Minimizing violence in the workplace

    d) Reducing CAUTI and CLABSI rates

    e) Health system transformation

10. Professional nursing organizations carry out which of the following functions:

    a) Organizing nurses into unions

    b) Providing a voice of nursing to legislators

    c) Educating nurses about advocacy

    d) Both b & c

    e) None of the above

# LEADERSHIP IN SOCIAL AND POLITICAL DETERMINANTS OF HEALTH

## REFLECTIVE QUESTIONS

1. Review the CDC website on Social Determinants of Health: https://www.cdc.gov/socialdeterminants/index.htm

   What SDOH effects have you seen regularly in your professional role? What are some current federal, state, or local healthcare policies that might address the issue?

   _____

   _____

   _____

   _____

   _____

   _____

2.   Why is it important to address both?

_____

_____

_____

_____

_____

3.   Why is it important for nurses to infuse loving-kindness as they use Unitary Caring Science approaches in their advocacy work?

_____

_____

_____

_____

_____

4.   Reflect on your own structural racism experiences and biases in healthcare that you have experienced or witnessed as a patient, a family member, or a provider. How can we begin to dismantle structural racism?

_____

_____

_____

_____

_____

_____

5.  Create a visual representation of the intersection of SPDH, Unitary Caring Science, and political advocacy. Prepare to discuss this or create a narrative around it.

    How are political determinants of health different from social determinants of health?

    _____

    _____

    _____

    _____

    _____

# NARRATIVE

A Black 47-year-old man living with heart failure (whom we will call Al) was enrolled in a research study at the local safety-net hospital. Al was hesitant to be involved with his cardiology team, and at enrollment into the research study with the research nurse and social worker, he talked about how he didn't trust healthcare. He shared that a family member of his was experimented on in the Tuskegee airmen experiments. Al felt his family had been experimented on enough throughout their history by healthcare professionals who were supposed to help them.

Al talked about how the historical impact of healthcare's inequitable treatment of minoritized groups like his family had made him so fearful of healthcare that he didn't get help for his severe edema, shortness of breath, and chest pain until he could no longer work because of the severity of his symptoms. He wasn't willing to have his heart failure more actively managed by his cardiology team. Because of his passive response to his illness, he had only ended up accessing care when he was in an emergency state. Al shared that he had joined the research study only to share his experience and wanted to make sure people weren't being experimented on as they had been in the past.

This is an example of how healthcare and policy created situations that exploited minoritized groups and destroyed trust with people who needed to be included and welcomed. This patient's historical experience with systematic oppression was directly impacting his relationship with his healthcare providers in the current day.

# RESPONSE TO THE NARRATIVE

1.  How would you approach caring for Al using a Unitary Caring Science and/or critical race theory perspective?

_____

_____

_____

_____

_____

_____

2.  Al's cardiology research team could have felt this man was "noncompliant" because he didn't follow up with his appointments or take his prescribed medications. How can you frame his actions from a Unitary Caring Science perspective that examines the SPDH of this situation?

_____

_____

_____

_____

_____

_____

3.  How would you share Al's experience with the cardiology research team?

_____

_____

_____

_____

_____

_____

4.  What does this example teach us about patients who are given labels like "noncompliant" or "difficult"? Using a critical race theory perspective, what are the underlying social constructs of systemic racism related to these labels and Al's experience?

_____

_____

_____

_____

_____

_____

_____

# QUIZ QUESTIONS

1.  The concept that all members of society should have the same basic rights, protection, opportunities, and social benefits is called:

    a) Diversity

    b) Equity

    c) Social justice

    d) All the above

2.  What is the difference between equality and equity?

    a) Equality is providing the same resources to everyone, while equity is providing help to only the worst-off communities.

    b) Equality provides needed resources tailored to each group, while equity provides the same resources to everyone.

    c) Equality is providing the same resources to everyone, while equity provides needed resources to each group.

    d) Equality provides resources to only the worst-off communities, while equity provides the same resources to everyone.

3.  How do diversity, equity, and inclusion improve nursing leadership?

    a) Creates trust with a community

    b) Improves the amount of work a team can get done

    c) More accurately represents the population nursing serves

    d) Both a & c

4.  How do diversity, equity, and inclusion improve the nursing discipline?

    a) Creates trust with a community

    b) Improves innovation and diversity of ideas

    c) Both a & b

    d) None of the above

5.  Social determinants of health are independent of stigma.

    a) True

    b) False

6.  A socioeconomically disadvantaged community experiencing pollution from a chemical plant is an example of a political determinant of health.

    a) True

    b) False

7.  How does the historical impact of inequitable policies impact healthcare?

    a) Inequitable policies do not influence healthcare.

    b) There are not historical inequities.

    c) By creating advantages for some groups and not for others, society limits individuals' ability to create healing and health.

    d) All the above

8.  Nurses can be very effective advocates and leaders in addressing SPDH because they understand the whole person.

    a) True

    b) False

9.  The base of Unitary Caring Science is centered on the nurse's impact on patient care.

    a) True

    b) False

10. The COVID-19 pandemic created health disparities that caused minoritized populations to suffer from more significant adverse health outcomes.

    a) True

    b) False

# 21

# CREATING A CONNECTED WORLD: A CALL TO ETHICS OF FACE AND BELONGING

## REFLECTIVE QUESTIONS

1.  How does the concept of an inflection point in business inform leaders' decision-making moving forward?

_____

_____

_____

_____

_____

_____

_____

2.  What role/function do white space, unusual suspects, and serendipity play as aspects of chaos theory?

_____

_____

_____

_____

_____

_____

3.  How might learning "to hold opposites or paradoxical concepts in the same space" help with decision-making in the delivery of healthcare?

_____

_____

_____

_____

_____

_____

4.  The affective domain is often called the "soft skills" domain. How has the pandemic affected healthcare providers' sense of purpose and meaning with the work they perform? Support your position.

_____

_____

_____

_____

_____

_____

_____

_____

5.  How do the concepts of white space, unusual suspects, and serendipity support diversity, equity, and inclusion initiatives?

_____

_____

_____

_____

_____

_____

# NARRATIVE

A large, vertically integrated health system with a Unitary Caring Science (UCS) affiliation identified a business need to increase the number of BSN-prepared nurses within its organization as part of the journey toward Magnet status. After conducting a review of the nursing workforce, the organization realized that its nursing workforce had a retention rate that remained relatively constant over the study period. Given that these nurses would remain with the organization until retirement, replacing them with BSN-prepared nurses was not going to accomplish the 80% target goal for the Magnet journey during their projected timeline. The organization had a longstanding academic-service partnership with a private local health sciences university. A proposal to create an RN-to-BSN program with a UCS foundation was made to this university. The proposal included significant tuition support for working nurses who wished to return to school to complete this degree. The program's stated ultimate objective was to change the nursing culture at this organization.

# RESPONSE TO THE NARRATIVE

How can the six human attributes of the 21st century Conceptual Age be integrated into both the educational and practice settings of these organizations to engage and ultimately retain nurses in the organization and/or profession?

# QUIZ QUESTIONS

1.  An inflection point, in a business context, is about gathering signals of business model assumptions from the edges of the interactions with clients where assumptions might be challenged.

    a) True

    b) False

2.  The utilization of white space, as applied in the business context, is about testing the assumptions of the original business model to the weak signals found at the edges of the current business delivery.

    a) True

    b) False

3.  Utilization of the "unusual suspects" part of chaos theory is about looking for those current stakeholders who are *not* usually included in decision-making in a given work unit.

    a) True

    b) False

4.  Utilization of diversity, equity, and inclusion (DEI) is about inviting those who are not accustomed to being part of a decision-making role into that process.

    a) True

    b) False

5.  Polarity management is about creating space to hold two disparate concepts in the same cognitive decision-making space.

    a) True

    b) False

6.  The six human attributes required of the Conceptual Age include:

    a) Design, Work, Story, Caring, Play, Meaning

    b) Design, Work, Story, Empathy, Play, Meaning

    c) Symphony, Design, Story, Empathy, Play, Meaning

    d) Symphony, Work, Empathy, Story, Play, Meaning

    e) Meaning, Play, Caring, Story, Design, Symphony

7.  Social determinants of health are non-medical factors that contribute to the health and well-being of an individual.

    a) True

    b) False

8.  The experience of discrimination is not considered a social determinant of health.

    a) True

    b) False

9.  Levinasian Ethics supports that in order to be, one must be gainfully employed.

    a) True

    b) False

10. Screening patients for SDOH is an upstream tactic employed to promote health.

    a) True

    b) False

11. The provision of direct care to patients is a downstream tactic.

    a) True

    b) False

12. Upstream tactics to promote health include the enactment of laws and regulations that have a broad impact on community well-being.

    a) True

    b) False